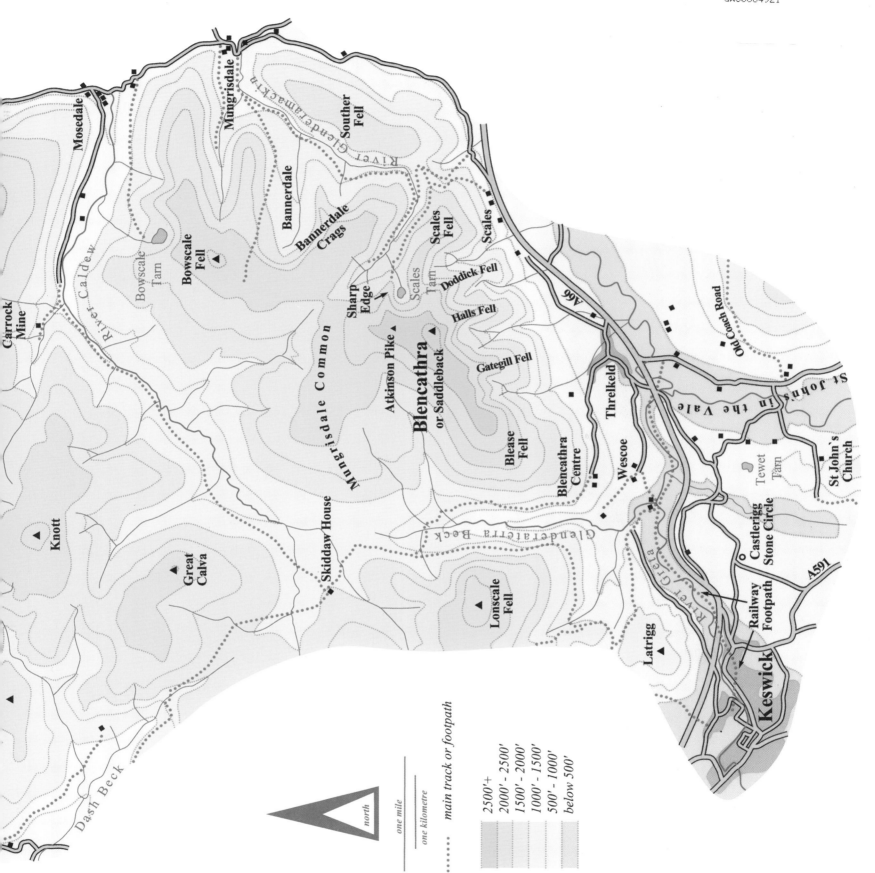

Mosedale

Mungrisdale

Souther Fell

Bannerdale

Bannerdale Crags

River Glenderamackin

Scales Fell

Scales

Carrock Mine

River Caldew

Bowscale Tarn

Bowscale Fell

Scales Tarn

Doddick Fell

Sharp Edge

Halls Fell

A66

Mungrisdale Common

Atkinson Pike

Blencathra or Saddleback

Gategill Fell

Threlkeld

Old Coach Road

Knott

Blease Fell

Blencathra Centre

Wescoe

St Johns in the Vale

Skiddaw House

Great Calva

Glenderaterra Beck

Tewet Tarn

St John's Church

Lonscale Fell

Castlerigg Stone Circle

River Greta

A591

Latrigg

Railway Footpath

Dash Beck

Keswick

north

one mile

one kilometre

· · · · · · main track or footpath

2500'+
2000' - 2500'
1500' - 2000'
1000' - 1500'
500' - 1000'
below 500'

BLENCATHRA

Portrait of a Mountain

THE FELL WITH EVERYTHING

For many walkers, Blencathra, standing above the busy A66 at the northeastern corner of Lakeland, is the finest fell of them all.

Which is odd. In terms of height above the sea it's only England's fourteenth – lower than the Scafells, lower even than Raise and Esk Pike and Pillar. It is also in the wrong place: the self-contained block north of the Vale of Keswick which is, by general consent, the least exciting end of Lakeland. The Northern Fells as a whole are more akin to the Pennines or Scotland's Southern Uplands. And within this rounded, grassy hill group, Blencathra is overshadowed by its big brother to the west, Skiddaw.

Being in the Northern Fells, Blencathra is even made of the wrong sort of rock. Pioneering photographers George and Ashley Abrahams took their first climbing pictures on the crags below Sharp Edge. The photos are impressive, but the climbing was horrible: steep, grassy and loose. Skiddaw Slate is not a rock-climbing rock, and those of the grab-and-dangle persuasion stay to the south of Derwent Water on the rugged rocks of the Central Fells.

Meanwhile those who, ever since the 18th century, have been disparagingly named as 'tourists', are trudging up Skiddaw by its wide and unexciting path. But for us who call ourselves walkers, the hill of splendour is Saddleback – or the name it usually goes by these days, Blencathra. By either name, and for what walkers want, this is the hill that has it all.

Blencathra stands steep-sided and solitary at the edge of that northern fell block of Lakeland. Its five front ridges rise from the village of Threlkeld straight to the sky, where they make crinkly shapes against the rushing grey clouds above.

The ordinary way up Blencathra is one of the most intriguing easy ascents in Lakeland. It passes through the low Mousthwaite col, along the steep side wall of an unsuspected back valley, then rises past waterfalls

Looking west from Gategill Top to Blease Fell. Across the cloud sea is Grasmoor.

into a perfect combe with black crags and a deep, cold tarn. This Scales Tarn route is steep only briefly, it winds through six different sorts of places, and it still manages to keep the summit view a secret until the very last minute. I like it as a descent, as the toes appreciate its non-steep nature even more when going downhill.

Many who call ourselves walkers will also want some easy scrambling. Blencathra has two Grade 1 scrambles, one mild and one tough within this easisest of the scrambling grades, but both of them tops for quality. Halls Fell is a real ridge. After its steep and heathery start, it rises as rocks for 400m of height gain, but nowhere is it at all difficult. It's suitable for an adventurous fellwalker over the age of eight, and any such short-legged walker will be distracted by the rock features into failing to notice many of those 400 metres of ascent. Sharp Edge on the other hand is exposed and serious, a narrow arete high above Scales Tarn. It's one of the finest, but also one of the hardest, Grade 1 scrambles in Lakeland.

The Scales Tarn route or one or other of the two scrambles, possibly followed by the uncomplicated descent by Blease Fell, makes most people's first expedition on Blencathra. But there's much, much more. The ridges on either side of Halls Fell are slightly less rocky, but a whole lot wilder. Or if you're feeling grumpy, the ravines between those ridges are full of scree, and sheep, and steep wet shale. Wainwright's *Pictorial Guide* devotes pages of polite but vivid disapproval to these routes. Less articulate walkers will resort to grunts and swear-words.

And then, for solitary wanderers, there's the Back o' Blencathra. Back o' Blencathra has Bowscale Fell and Bannerdale Crags, both with genuine craggy bits. Bowscale Fell has another classic tarn, and beyond it is the heap of gabbro, granite and gorse called Carrock Fell. Back o' Blencathra with its sterile underlying slates is a comparatively poor place for mountain wildflowers, but across the scoured sides of Carrock can be found a dozen strange sorts of

Saddleback and the Alps: 'whimsical and disgusting' mountains, as portrayed by William Gilpin in 1786. Book illustration courtesy of Carlisle Library.

SADDLEBACK: THE WRONG SHAPE

Our game of going up hills and looking at the view goes back, ultimately, to an 18th-century vicar called William Gilpin. He invented 'Picturesque Beauty', and published the first handbooks for its appreciation. For him, Saddleback was not only in the wrong place and of the wrong sort of stone. It was also quite the wrong shape.

"In the mean time, with all this magnificence and beauty, it cannot be supposed, that every scene, which these countries present, is correctly picturesque. In such immense bodies of rough-hewn matter, many irregularities, and even many deformities, must exist, which a practised eye would wish to correct....

"The pyramidal shape, and easy flow of an irregular line, will be found in the mountain, as in other delineations, the truest source of beauty. Mountains therefore rising in regular, mathematical lines, or in whimsical, grotesque shapes, are displeasing. Thus Burnswark, a mountain on the southern border of Scotland; Thorpe-Cloud, near Dovedale in Derbyshire, especially when seen from the garden at Ilam; and a mountain in Cumberland, which from it's peculiar appearance in some situations, takes the name of Saddleback, all form, disagreeable lines. And thus many of the pointed summits of the Alps are objects rather of singularity than of beauty. Such forms also as suggest the idea of lumpish heaviness are disgusting – round, swelling forms, without any break to disincumber them of their weight."

Observations, relative chiefly to Picturesque Beauty, Made in the Year 1772, On several Parts of England; particularly the Mountains, and Lakes of Cumberland, and Westmoreland
– William Gilpin 1786

The Northern Fells seen across the Solway from Castle Point,
Kirkcudbrightshire. At far left, Carrock Fell; then the Back
o' Skiddaw, with high points at High Pike and Great Calva.
Skiddaw dominates the right-hand side of the group, with
Blencathra half-hidden behind it on the left. At the left-hand end
of Blencathra's summit plateau, the steep top of Sharp Edge can
be seen quite clearly even from this distance of over 50km (30
miles).

FOLLOWING PAGES: The reverse view: Skiddaw (left) and
Blencathra seen across Derwent Water and the Vale of Keswick.
The pointed hill in the foreground is Catbells.

'It is said to be so deep, that the
sun never shines upon it, and that
the reflection of the stars may be
seen therein at noon-day'

*The Saddle of Saddleback,
seen at daybreak from just
south of Berrier. We look
directly into the hollow
of Scales Tarn, enclosed
between Scales Fell (left) and
Sharp Edge. Greenah Crag
Farm is in the foreground.*

1. SCALES TARN AND SHARP EDGE

BLENCATHRA: GATEGILL TOP · BLENCATHRA: HALLS FELL · SCALES FELL · ATKINSON PIKE · SHARP EDGE · SOUTHER FELL · BANNERDALE CRAGS

BLENCATHRA THE SCALES WAY

The curious crater and lake there, where the lava of a volcano is unquestionably to be found in large quantities
– Hutchinson's *History of Cumberland* (1794)

Very few fellwalks unfold quite so delightfully as the ascent of Blencathra by way of Mousthwaite Comb, Scales Tarn, and Scales Fell. It's a route that reveals itself step by step, almost like a sonnet.

The walk starts, it's true, rather steeply. The path climbs the shallow, half-open Mousthwaite Comb in a spiralling curve. Behind, the view widens across the fields and farms of Glenderamackin, with the pudding-like hump of Great Mell Fell and a glimpse along the Ullswater valley. But before you can get more than slightly tired, you find yourself at the Mousthwaite col. And here, a new little world opens out.

Before you, the ground drops into a little river valley. It's the Glenderamackin again, as it happens, much further up in its winding course. The path bends half-left up this unexpected hollow, and continues almost level along the steep side wall, high above the stream. Behind, the lowlands are now only a glimpse through the notch of the col. As you move up the valley, that first view of the walk is forgotten, as your eye is drawn upwards by the rock tower that's the beginning of Sharp Edge.

This enclosed and gentle second section continues for about a mile. Then the path crosses the Scales Beck and turns abruptly uphill. This is steep, and the footing is sometimes bare rock. Attention is divided between the path itself and the succession of small waterfalls alongside. You'll probably be ignoring the wider landscape over this stretch; which is a neat literary trick played on you by the path itself. For the angle eases; and suddenly over the space of a few steps, half a mile of water opens out in front of you.

Scales Tarn and its combe are the textbook example of a glaciated corrie hollow. What the textbook doesn't mention is the texture of the headwall: bright with grassy terraces and tiny streams. It doesn't mention the steep line of the scree as it tumbles to the water, and on under the water to invisible depths. It bluntly summarises as 'glacial arete' the cheerful crinkles of Sharp Edge high on the right.

It's only fair to say that Wainwright, referring to the route so far – Mousthwaite Comb, the Glenderamackin, Scales Beck – describes it as "a rather dreary line of approach". Wainwright is rarely wrong but on this occasion I think he was distracted. He was using this path as an approach to Sharp Edge, and all the way along it, was probably worrying about that scrambly bit to come.

From Scales Tarn there are two ways onwards. The first of them is that exciting scramble of Sharp Edge, which forms the arete high on the right. The easier continuation is a steep path rising from the tarn's back left corner onto the summit plateau. I like to ignore both of them. Instead, at the tarn's outflow I turn up the grassy slope on the left. This is pathless, and quite steep, but it brings you onto the crest of Scales Fell.

And here is the walk's final transformation. Ahead, the ground drops suddenly in scree and heather: you're looking again at the walk's first view, the one southwards towards Ullswater – but quite altered by the 2000ft of height you've gained since you last saw it. Now you turn right and head up the ridge path, passing the tops of the various ridges and ravines of Blencathra's southern face. On the right, you look across the deep hole of Scales Tarn to the jags and notches of Sharp Edge. Beyond it there rises into sight the rounded moorland fells of the Back o' Skiddaw; and beyond them again, the Solway Firth and possibly even Scotland.

Ahead, the zigzags of an engineered path lead up to the summit plateau. The walk, sadly, is almost over. So let's go back and do it all over again, this time in the year 1793…

Hutchinson's *History of Cumberland* of 1794 gives a hearsay account of an ascent of Blencathra in 1793, guided by Thomas Clement of Scales. The party of three plus guide set off up Scales Fell.

"When we had ascended about a mile, one of the party, on looking round, was so astonished with the different appearance of objects in the valley, so far beneath us, that he declined proceeding. We had not gone much further, till the other companion was suddenly taken ill, and wished to lose blood, and return. I was almost ready to give up my project, which I should have done with great reluctance, as the day was remarkably favourable, and exhibited every scene to the greatest advantage.—Mr Clement assured us,

Scales Tarn at dawn, with Sharp Edge on the right

Mousthwaite col (left) and the path along the steep side of the Glenderamackin.

if we proceeded a little way, we should find a resting place, where the second defaulter of our party might recover the effects of his journey. After labouring another half hour, we gained the margin of an immense cavity, in the side of the mountain, the bottom of which formed a wide bason, and was filled with water, that from our station looked black, though smooth as glass, covering the space of several acres. It is said to be so deep, that the sun never shines upon it, and that the reflection of the stars may be seen therein at noon-day; but that was a curiosity we did not enjoy….

We now contemplated the scene with *awestruck wonder*.—We stood directly facing the middle of the mountain, the form of which gives it the name of *Saddleback:* and to the lake a perpendicular rocky precipice presented itself, extending to the north-east side of the mountain, called Foul-crag. To the right hand the steepness of the rocks gradually declined ; above us, and on the left, they were stupendous and perpendicular ; so that

in one half of the circle the rocks were lofty and precipitous, whilst in the other half they gradually decreased. My fellow traveller would proceed no further ; and, with my guide, I was left to explore the other parts of the mountain. Winding round, and keeping the cavity on our right, we attained the ridge or summit of the rock, where we found a passage three or four yards broad: on the right, the descent to the lake looked truly awful ; whilst the steep rocks on the other side were lofty, and not to be climbed by human steps. This passage, some hundred yards in length, may be compared to a bridge covered with grass."

After enjoying the summit view, the two surviving party members crossed the plateau to Foule Crag, and daringly skirted the slope above Sharp Edge:

from whence we looked down into a dreadful abyss, the bottom of which the eye could not penetrate: sheep frequently perish in this place, as the number of dead carcasses and skeletons

Dawn view back over the Mousthwaite col to Great Mell Fell

evinced… To look down from thence was so terrible, I could not endure it for a moment.

At this point the cloud came down briefly, but the brave pair managed to find Scales Fell and the abandoned companion. They can't have spent too much time trembling on the various brinks, as the ascent and descent together took just four hours.

It's easy to ridicule these early explorers for managing to achieve altitude sickness at only 800m. But in the 18th century, you were a poor sort of fellwalker if you *weren't* struck down by terror and amazement. The most elevated sort of landscape experience was one with a certain amount of scariness, or in the jargon of the time, the sublime.

A handbook to all this was written by up-and-coming philosopher Edmund Burke (*A Philosophical Enquiry into the Sublime and Beautiful,* 1757). He explains in detail what we are supposed to feel: not terror as such, but "astonishment; and astonishment is that state of the soul, in which all its motions are suspended, with some degree of horror" – and he praises this as "the strongest emotion which the mind

is capable of feeling". He helpfully then explains in detail where to find such feelings. Not in bright sunlight, but in shade and obscurity; not in civilised scenes, but in danger and difficulty, in solitude and in silence. The Sublime is found in darkness, hugeness, and in vast empty spaces.

These travellers with their tremors and their vertigo are simply demonstrating their sophistication in this fashionable art.

That's not to say it wasn't, at the same time, ridiculous. As early as 1801, Jane Austen was ridiculing it in *Sense and Sensibility.* Seventeen-year-old Marianne Dashwood is a 'New Romantic' of the early 19th century: "Thomson, Cowper, Scott—she would buy them all; and she would have every book that tells her how to admire a twisted old tree." And so she gets gently 'teazed' [Austen spelling] by Edward Ferrars.

"I have no knowledge in the picturesque, and I shall offend you by my ignorance and want of taste. I shall call hills steep, which ought to be bold; surfaces strange and uncouth,

ABOVE: Scales Tarn and Sharp Edge.
OPPOSITE: A pre-dawn view of Sharp Edge from the path above the Glenderamackin River

FOLLOWING PAGES: Three walkers on the final stage of Scales Fell, starting the final slope to Blencathra's summit plateau.

which ought to be irregular and rugged; and distant objects out of sight, which ought to be indistinct through the soft medium of a hazy atmosphere… I am not fond of nettles, or thistles, or heath blossoms. A troop of tidy, happy villagers pleases me better than the finest banditti in the world."

At the same time, William Wordsworth was giving (notably in *Tintern Abbey*) a more considered critique of what he called the "craving for a prospect", the collecting of views as if they were oil paintings by Salvator Rosa, to hang on your chamber wall and impress your friends with your arty tendencies.

The Romantics – the Wordsworths, William and Dorothy; Coleridge; sidekicks Southey and Lamb and de Quincey – brought a new way of going up hills. Their mountains were made of actual rock and earth. They walked up them attempting to see what was actually there, if also to see what was invisible behind what was actually there. And they enjoyed storms, sunrises, and the actual exercise of foot on foothold. Wordsworth himself paid little attention to Blencathra; this is possibly because his friend and rival Coleridge lived at the bottom of it. Coleridge descended the corrie headwall to Scales Tarn in August 1800, experienced neither altitude sickness nor attacks of panic, simply being within the scenery with his usual passionate absorption.

"Descend northward, and ascend, and thence see the Tarn: a round basin of vast depth, the west arc an almost perpendicular precipice of naked shelving crags (each crag a precipice with a small shelf). To the east the outlet. Northwest between a narrow chasm a little sike wound down over very green moss. At every fall the water fell off in little liquid icicles from the points of moss jelly bags—in one place a semi-round stone with sixteen of these. The northern wall of the basin green with huge scars of bare blue stone dust, and whiter stones. No noise but that of loose stones rolling away from the feet of the sheep, that move slowly along these perilous ledges."

Again, three years later (in September 1803) with Robert Southey: "through Threlkeld, up Saddleback, over Blenkarthur having the horse road a great deal to our right, to Saddleback Tarn. I had quite forgotten the fearfully sublime precipice and striding edge on its farther or northern side, and the colours of this little tarn: blood-crimson, and then sea-green, etc., etc., and so go on in sections, now calms, now ruffled spaces. Nowhere where more beautiful can you see the breeze-race, blowing a rich blue like the peacock's neck over the tarn, till where it comes near the blood-crimson, and then it turns the most beautiful purple."

In July 1831 the philosopher John Stuart Mill walked up what he calls 'Blencathara' by this route: and observed Scales Tarn with almost Wordsworthian intensity – he had in fact called on the Wordsworths a few days earlier.

We saw below us, in a nook, surrounded on three sides by heights as precipitous as turf will grow on, the beautiful tarn; we descended to its brink: it was the first genuine tarn that we had seen in these mountains (I had seen others in the Pyrenees), and we could not take our eyes off it. The water, which is of the deepest blue, seems hid, out of the reach of man; no trees or shrubs, nor even the smallest herb, overshadow it, yet one wonders at having found it, and deems it a prodigy that it should not have been overlooked. It is beautifully clear; a part of it is shallow, but it deepens suddenly; some light green moss-like weeds shew themselves at the bottom, but it is said to contain no fish. Its situation, and its little extent compared with the heights that overlook it, remind one of the pure crystalline water which collects in the basin formed by the united leaves of the teazle,

TOP: The zig-zag path on Scales Fell was constructed around 2002 by a small digger lifted in by helicopter. It replaced a 15m-wide eroded scar: even so, some walkers criticise these engineering works as intrusive.

MIDDLE: On the lower part of Scales Fell, walker and Collie silhouetted against the headwall of Scales Tarn – the tarn itself out of sight down right

BOTTOM: Dawn walker on Scales Fell, seen from Scales Tarn.

FOLLOWING PAGES: Half way up Scales Fell, at the point where the direct path from Scales Tarn reaches the ridge line. The view is down Doddick Fell to the Glenderamackin and Great Mell Fell.

"The two lakes, the vale, the river, and mountain mists, and clouds and sunshine make endless combinations as if heaven and earth were for ever talking to each other."

2. THE VALE OF KESWICK

THRELKELD, ST JOHN'S AND CASTLERIGG

BLENCATHRA: DODDICK FELL

GREAT MELL FELL

CLOUGH HEAD

THRELKELD GRANITE QUARY

THRELKELD

THIRLMERE

ST. JOHN'S CHURCH

BRIGHT TARN

CASTLERIGG STONE CIRCLE

DERWENT WATER

The two lakes, the vale, the river, and mountain mists, and clouds and sunshine make endless combinations as if heaven and earth were for ever talking to each other.
– Samuel Taylor Coleridge, letter from Greta Hall 1800

Three miles from Keswick on the right is a good family house called Burns, whence on the descent to the river Greta or Bure is in view on the right the mountains of St. John's, and on the left Saddleback, here and several miles in advance displayed in a series of bold, square, and finely broken lines, which for their highly varied combinations of the picturesque, are unequalled in the country.
– William Green *Guide to the Lakes* 1818

Blencathra stands steep-sided and solitary at the southern edge of Lakeland's northern fells. The Scafells are hidden above foothills, or rise at the ends of long, twisting valleys. Even Skiddaw lies back from the Bassenthwaite plains. No hill in England (with the possible exception of the Malverns) rises so steep and stark out of the populated lowlands as Blencathra does. Ever since the glacier shovelled its great gap and then melted away, the Vale of Keswick has been a wide band of field and settlement in the middle of the hills.

Slightly up the side of that wide valley, just above what were once the bogs of the valley floor, sprawls the small village of Threlkeld. Above its topmost gardens the great riven wall of Blencathra rises almost alarmingly. The ancient stonework of Threlkeld's main street bends under the weight of ages; the Horse and Farrier Inn is marked with the date 1688, the year of the Spanish Armada. According to the barman, it was an inn from the beginning: "Older as well as better than the other place" – the Salutation Inn across the road. But both buildings must be considered as intrusions of modernity in a settlement originally of the Norsemen: the name means 'Thrall's Spring', a thrall being a serf or slave.

A century ago, the Horse and Farrier was the fox-hunters' pub, while the Salutation was preferred by the lead workers from the Gategill mines just above the village. Today, both inns are decorated with hunting scenes. Whether or not we believe the barman, the horror story writer Ann Radcliffe stayed at the Horse

Blencathra across the Greta valley, seen from Walla Crag. The Blencathra Centre lies just below the bracken on the leftmost summit, Blease Fell: houses further downhill are Wescoe. At the far right of the picture.

and Farrier in 1794, finding the facilities basic but the staff friendly. Wordsworth and Coleridge, on the walking tour that was Coleridge's first visit to Lakeland, spent the night of 15th November 1799 at Threlkeld. So it was probably in this very building that they picked up the legend of Henry Clifford, the shepherd aristocrat, wandering at the back of Blencathra. Wordsworth's poem on the legend will be quoted in a later section.

Two lanes run west out of the village, along Blencathra's flank. The lower leads to Wescoe, where the poet WH Auden stayed. The upper leads to the Blencathra Centre, a former sanatorium for tuberculosis sufferers, briefly a general hospital, and now a field centre for an educational charity. Hugh Walpole's novel *The Bright Pavilions*, set in early Elizabethan times, has its witch-burning "on a plateau half-way up the mountain" in a clearing of the brushwood – the description fits the present location of Blencathra Centre as well as anywhere. Written during the war, it's a grimmer piece than his better-known Herries chronicles, though with a Herries protagonist.

It's on April 14th 1586, that the novel's Frau Hodstetter, from the German mining community, is burned on Blencathra. "The mountain's thin ridge – the Saddleback – stood sharp and clear against the faint green sky in which the pared moon was struggling against whispy clouds… Above the sparse brushwood immediately in front of them a pale rosy light hung against the sky, rising and falling as though blown by a bellows."

Gilbert Armstrong saves the witch's daughter Catherine by claiming her as his fiancée – he does this because his master, Nicholas Herries, is hopelessly in love with Catherine. But the aroused mob immediately carries them both down to Crosthwaite Church and forcibly marries them.

A site on Skiddaw – perhaps Latrigg – would have been much more convenient for Walpole's witch-burners. From the closest corner of Blencathra it's three full miles to Keswick and Crosthwaite. Three reasons suggest themselves as to why Walpole sent his mob all the way to Blencathra to burn his witch. He may have wished not to echo Macaulay's "The red glare on Skiddaw roused the burghers of Carlisle" – that poem on the Spanish Armada being an irrelevance here. Or, the specific date given suggests Walpole may be referring to an actual or legendary event remembered in Keswick. Thirdly, he may have followed the now rejected derivation of Blencathra as 'Chair of the Devil'.

While Walpole's witch-burners, and Satan squatting on Saddleback, are probably just stories,

in the first half of the 18th century, the good souls of Threlkeld were in the care of a vicar as eccentric as any to have graced the Church of England.

The Rev Alexander Naughley actually arrived as a refugee from the Church of Scotland – entering Threlkeld in a pony pannier led by his father, an Episcopalian evicted by Presbyterian persecutions. The younger Naughley was noted as a mathematician and astronomer – but even more for his austere lifestyle. According to a footnote in Hutchinson's *History of Cumberland* (1794), he lived only on crusts of bread, along with oatmeal porridge boiled in a single saucepan that was never washed. "His dress was only comparable to his diet: it was, in general, the meanest and worst in the parish. He always wore wooden shoes, and went without cravat, stock, or handkerchief round his neck: his slovenliness will not bear description. His hearth was seldom cleared of the embers; whilst his whole apartment was strewed over with books and papers, intermingled with his household implements."

However, the reason he was vividly remembered 50 years after his death was down to his literal interpretation of one particular verse of the New Testament. At Matthew xix 12, Jesus suggests: "For there are some eunuchs, which were so born from their mother's womb: and there are some eunuchs, which were made eunuchs of men: and there be eunuchs, which have made themselves eunuchs for the kingdom of heaven's sake." According to my informant in today's Church of England this is interpreted metaphorically, as precious things generally that must be snipped away. Naughley is one of only three Christians known to have taken it as written. Origen of Alexandria did the same self-snipping in the 3rd century. Thomas Boston Corbett took a pair of scissors to himself in 1858, and is also known as the man who killed President Lincoln's assassin, John Wilkes Booth.

The Vicar of Threlkeld's operation wasn't altogether successful. "After this act of self-violence, he became sottish, grovelling, and mean in the extreme; unstudious, and without either ambition or effort to improve his understanding. His voice also was rendered so effeminate, weak, and piping, that his congregation, even when they could hear him at all, no longer heard him with pleasure."

In the 19th century Threlkeld thrived as copper and lead were extracted from the slopes of Blencathra just above. It has a small but handsome Victorian village hall, as well as a housing estate so new that, while I was taking pictures of the village, it still boasted a hoarding displaying the happy family soon to be inhabiting the cosy sofas and tightly fitted

At the end of a long day in Lakeland, the pulloff at the Mungrisdale road end often provides a final photo opportunity.

Castlerigg Stone Circle

kitchens. The grinning family in its casual attire looked incongruous below the high grey slope of Blencathra.

RUDE STONES OF THE DRUIDS

"These interesting memorials of the primeval age of Britain consist of forth-eight rude, unhewn blocks of granite, thirty-eight of which are disposed in an oval figure, of which the diameter is thirty-four yards from north to south, and nearly thirty from east to west…

The situation of this place for superstitious worship has been skilfully chosen, when considered with reference to the idolatrous superstitions of the Druids; the objects of which were to subdue the mind with appalling images, and to extort obedience through the agency of terror. It is seated in the neighbourhood of Skiddaw, Blencathara, and Helvellyn… whose clouded summits impended over the sacrificial altar, casting obscure shadows through its precincts. Hither the trembling worshippers repaired, to hear and to acknowledge the teachings and denunciations of their potent masters. In the eyes of the barbarian Britons, alike ignorant, credulous, and superstitious, the place would appear to be the very sanctuary of Omnipotence, and the Druid ministers themselves an impersonation of their gods. Wind and cloud, storm and tempest, wrought powerfully in the abstruse mysteries and terrific incantations constituting the Druidical worship ; and the mind was prostrated, with terrific awe, at the shrine where natural sublimity combined with human cunning to thrill its scarcely awakened faculties." – Lorenzo Tuvar *Tales & Legends of the English Lakes & Mountains* (1852). (Tuvar goes on to recite the story of Ella, a charming young prehistoric maiden about to be burned to death at midwinter in a ritualistic wicker hut – when floods of water burst out of fissures in the rock and extinguish the fire. Meanwhile a dreadful voice announces to the Arch-Druid that the Year Zero has arrived, and the Mystic Rites racket is being taken over by the Baby Jesus).

Half way along the great valley gap, and midway between its high hill sides, stands the stone circle of Castlerigg. This is perhaps the third most spectacular stonework on the UK mainland (after Stonehenge and Avebury). Anyone who knows what it was built for is almost certainly fooling themselves. Coleridge's intuition could be as close as we'll get: it honours the spirit of the place. Those who claim to decipher mystical alignments might note Coleridge's cryptic note of November 1799: "NB The Keswickians have been playing tricks with the stones." Teasingly, he adds no details of this rumour.

Druidical and New Age characters gather here

ABOVE: Signpost at the Old Coach Road's western end, where it joins the tarred road through St John's Vale. The old road is still technically a public highway, and is signed as a road rather than a footpath.
TOP LEFT: The old road runs below Wolf Crags, with Clough Head ahead.
BOTTOM LEFT: Looking eastwards along the old road as it rises out of St John's Vale. Ahead, the Pennines rise beyond Penrith, with Great Mell Fell to the right.

at the summer solstice. At other times it is fairly quiet; perhaps a couple of people with cameras and a dozen or so sheep may be wandering among the standing stones. It certainly isn't on a par with, say, Beatrix Potter's place at High Sawrey. But for the early visitors the 'druidical temple' was one of Lakeland's must-see spots on the way in to West's eight essential viewpoints around Derwent Water. West's guidebook of 1778 calls it a "wide circus of rude stones; the awful monument of the barbarous superstition which enslaved the minds of ancient times".

Rude here means rough and unsophisticated; the shapes of the stones are not especially obscene. Today we are flooded with images of everywhere. From an impulse to view Stonehenge, it has just taken me 18 seconds to bring up an image of it. But Gray and Wordsworth might behold Stonehenge just once or twice in a lifetime; and they gave Castlerigg the attention it deserves.

Despite being one of the Lakes Poets, in 1824 Robert Southey claimed the stroll from Keswick to the Druidical Stones as not just his favourite but his only Lakeland fellwalk. In the third of his *Colloquies on the Progress and Prospects of Society*, he claims that:

> Inclination would lead me to hibernate during half the year in this uncomfortable climate of Great Britain, where few men who have tasted the enjoyments of a better would willingly take up their abode … I envy the Turks for their sedentary constitutions, which seem no more to require exercise than an oyster does or a toad in a stone. In this respect, I am by disposition as true a Turk as the Grand Seignior himself; and approach much nearer

to one in the habit of inaction than any person of my acquaintance…

> On a grey sober day, therefore, and in a tone of mind quite accordant with the season, I went out unwillingly to take the air… Even on such occasions as this, it is desirable to propose to oneself some object for the satisfaction of accomplishing it, and to set out with the intention of reaching some fixed point, though it should be nothing better than a mile-stone, or a directing post. So I walked to the Circle of Stones on the Penrith road, because there is a long hill upon the way which would give the muscles some work to perform.

His purpose in the *Colloquy* is to meet up with the ghost of Sir Thomas More. In opposition to the wisdom of the time, they discuss how much happier and healthier the rude Druids were than the miserable degenerates of the 1820s.

The historian Macaulay considered this as the very worst thing Southey ever wrote: "It would be scarcely possible for a man of Mr. Southey's talents and acquirements to write two volumes so large as those before us, which should be wholly destitute of information and amusement." Strong sentiments, when considering the author of the truly dreadful *You are Old, Father William* – though Southey did also write *Goldilocks and the Three Bears*.

"What if your manufactures, according to the ominous opinion which your greatest physiologist has expressed, were to generate for you new physical plagues, as they have already produced a moral pestilence unknown to all preceding ages?" In the *Colloquy*, as well as this prophesy of global warming, Southey has some useful notes on Castlerigg: "Concerning this, like all similar monuments in Great Britain, the popular superstition prevails, that no two persons can number the stones alike, and that no person will ever find a second counting confirm the first. My children have often disappointed their natural inclination to believe this wonder, by putting it to the test and disproving it. The number of the stones which compose the circle, is thirty-eight."

Southey thus enters this book as its token non-fellwalker. Or he would do, but for the fact that in September 1803 he walked with Coleridge from Keswick to Caldbeck over several summits including Blencathra.

The poet John Keats visited the stone circle in June 1818 in particularly favourable circumstances: at dusk, and exhausted. Starting at 4am, he had already walked from Wythburn on Thirlmere to Keswick before breakfast, followed by a circuit of Derwent

THRELKELD

ABOVE: The Horse and Farrier, Threlkeld.
LEFT: A single sunflower makes an unusual plant choice for a hanging basket, in the village which regularly features in the 'Cumbria in Bloom' awards.

FOLLOWING PAGES: Derwent Water from Jenkin Hill.

BLENCATHRA – FOR BEGINNERS

Where in the Lakes do you take a couple of children who've never done Lakeland before, but are pretty sure they're not going to like it? Grown-ups go up a stony slope for two or three hours, crouch behind a cairn peeling oranges with cold fingers, and come back down again on sore feet – and then persuade themselves they've had an awe-inspiring tussle with the elements.

But kids are realists. Children don't even get to that windswept cairn. Children stop after half an hour and say they're tired now, and they propose to eat the oranges right away and then go back down. They aren't tired at all, they could keep going all day if they could see some reason to do so. But it takes more than a mere parent to persuade them.

However, Blencathra's Halls Fell Ridge might just do the trick. Blencathra's trick is this: it starts as nasty as they get – stony, loose, and relentlessly steep. And then, when you've done about a third of it and can't see how you're going to bear another two-thirds, it turns into a rocky crest. Rocky crest bears the same relation to hillwalking as computer games do to

computer-assisted learning. Technically speaking, Halls Fell is hillwalking; but it feels as if it isn't. You only have to do the first three hundred metres of Blencathra. The rest of the mountain just does itself.

Well, that's the theory. But daughter-aged-eight scrambles up the first of the rocks, stops at the top and bursts into tears. Was this a big mistake? No; but it was a small one. I've failed to point out the Path Round the Side. Like the guardian angel at the bed-foot, the path consoles simply by being there; while the rocks are what we actually go up on. On either side, steep heather plunges into stream valleys that really are quite a long way below. Back down the ridge there's an aerial view of the A66 and the field patterns of Threlkeld.

Bravely straight up the front is, here, the easy way to go – but I refrain from pointing a moral so dangerously not applicable to Real Life away from Blencathra. The ridge hauls us rapidly upwards and deposits us like a lift set for 'roof' at the very summit cairn. "Is that it?" asks son-aged-ten – not what children, or even grown-ups, usually want to know at the top of a 750-metre ascent.

The way down is even more important than the way up. Walking up's tiring but walking down hurts. Coming down Halls Fell Ridge is fun in running shoes – but family members who aren't prepared to enjoy hills unless they're actually enjoyable need a better way off Blencathra.

And this lies to hand – or to foot – on the grassy east ridge of Scales Fell, which curls down into what's technically a glaciated hanging valley with ice-plucked floor; and actually, Scales Tarn. The path goes down beside – or if you prefer, inside – the small splashy stream, then wanders along the high side of the Glenderamackin valley, which is almost as long as its name. This level section is important. The relentless descent, turning out to be even worse than going up was: that is what makes a mountain like Great Gable so particularly mean and horrible. Walk back around the bottom of Blencathra, looking down on farmhouse and A66, up at Halls Fell, now named as Our Ridge, being spiky against the sky.

SIX RIDGES OF SADDLEBACK

What walkers like is ridges, and Saddleback has six of them. Two of the six are Sharp Edge and Hall's Fell. These are so good that many walkers ignore altogether the other four.

Look at Saddleback from Clough Head or the Old Coach Road below, and it has a very simple layout. It's a rectangular face, 600m high and two kilometers wide, stony and steep. Four streams cut into the face, and three sharp little ridges come down between

ABOVE: Near the foot of the rocky section of Halls Fell.
OPPOSITE: High on Halls Fell Ridge, with a clouded glimpse towards Helvellyn.

the streams. At the two ends, two more ridges curve down gently like the arms of a cosy sofa. That's five ridges, and round the back on the right, fortunately out of sight, is the sixth and most fearsome, Sharp Edge.

They used to do these ridges as a fell race. The race went both up and down all five of the front ridges – but not Sharp Edge, that would be too silly. This race was never particularly popular, and was informal even by the standards of fell-running. One year the two usual race marshals (one at the top, one at the bottom) didn't arrive, and one of the runners' wives checked them off from inside the bar of the Horse and Farrier. The weather was particularly nasty that year, and it must have been difficult indeed to leave the cosy bar for the fourth or fifth ascent of Blencathra. At any rate, Colin Valentine won the race by being the only runner to finish it.

The right-hand sofa arm is Scales Fell. The roundabout route to this by Scales Tarn was celebrated in the opening section. There's a more direct path, straight up from the Mousthwaite col, that's gently grassy and makes a good way down Blencathra, even in the dark.

The next one along, Doddick Fell, has all the advantages of Halls Fell except for the rocky crest. There are one or two very easy rocks at the top; what leads up to them is a heather crest and a little path. Even the steep bit at the bottom isn't particularly steep. On any other mountain, Doddick Fell would be a famous and popular ascent route. If Halls Fell's a bit too difficult, then do Doddick.

The central ridgeline, above and just to east of Threlkeld village, is Halls Fell. It can, of course, be climbed even without children. Especially good is Halls Fell when cloud washes around among the pinnacles, and you look back down the ridge to rock towers fading one below the other, and the odd grey frozen rock-pool. But better still is Halls Fell when the ridge rises out of that cloud into sunlight; and there's a view of Helvellyn's snow-covered dome, with distant tops like icebergs floating in the southwest.

Half way up Gategill Fell there's a place called Knott Halloo. It's as nice as its name – a brief horizontal ridge of grass and gently rounded rock. There are little hollows to linger in, and lots and lots of grey mist to look at; it's a place of refuge in the stony face of Saddleback. You can get to Knott Halloo by coming all the way down the steep and rather nasty slope from the summit plateau. If you don't like that idea, then you can come all the way up the steep and rather nasty slope from the bottom.

The westernmost ridge is Blease Fell. Blease is easy – indeed Blease is a breeze, a wide grass slope with a rough path that becomes a newly built zigzag one for the final climb. It's too easy a route to do as an ascent of big Blencathra. But linger on the

Halls Fell Ridge late in a February day, refrozen after a thaw (left). Descending Halls Fell Ridge (right).

Near the foot of Doddick Fell

summit as the sun goes lower, and golden. The wind drops, the people have gone away, it's all very quiet. Rumpled cloud covers the Solway, but Skiddaw has emerged into the late light. At the other end of the summit ridge, Clough Head comes and goes among coloured clouds.

Having wandered to both ends of Blencathra and back, there might not be enough daylight to get down … But off the end of Blease Fell, the path ambles in wide, well-built zigzags that you may once have condemned as an intrusive urban pavement but that now save needing the torch in the half-darkness. Westwards beyond the Vale of Keswick, the iceberg-line of tops is floating against a sky going turquoise, below clouds going pink, above other clouds going purple. Far below, Derwent Water reflects the last of the sky colours, the A66 is a line of bright beads on a string, and the orange streetlights of Keswick are coming on one by one.

From the Blencathra Centre to Scales, a path above the fell wall conveniently links the bases of all five of the ridge routes. And as you pass the bottom of Blease Gill, if it does happen still to be daylight there's something else you notice. Ridges are not the only routes. There's a whole new day to do, going up and down the little stream valleys between.

And this is why Blencathra is for ever. Go up this mountain five times, and all you find is four more ways to go up it again.

TOP: Halls Fell
LEFT: Gategill Fell
RIGHT: Doddick Fell

Halls Fell Ridge, at the foot of the rocky section

THE BROCKEN SPECTRE

Halls Fell rises out of cloud into sunlight, on a low-sun January afternoon. When a wisp of cloud gathered in the hollow between me and the mountain, and the Brocken Spectre appeared in all its glory, I simply turned half-right and snapped its photo.

From the east early on, from the west in the afternoon, the low winter sun strikes Halls Fell crosswise either way: the hollow of Doddick Gill or of Gate Gill quite often traps warm damp air and a consequent cloud. Halls Fell is the only place where I've met the Spectre on two different days.

The spectre is named after the Brocken, which is the high point of the Harz Mountains of northern Germany. (It's 1141m high if you don't count the red-and-white striped radio tower, which adds a further 123m.) Coleridge, as it happens, climbed the Brocken in 1799. He records that the ghostly figure of yourself that you see carries, if you look very closely, a notice with the names of all those who have cursed you with "May you be carried to the top of the Brocken" – apparently considered by Germans of 1799 as a bad place to be.

Almost everybody who meets the spectre, recognises it for what it is: a shadow, cast upon the cloud. For one thing, when you wave at it, it waves back. Because the shadow is cast on many water drops at many different distances, it's only coherent when looking directly down the sunbeams. So you only see your own shadow, and any companion standing right beside you – but it's your own shadow that has the wide, multicoloured halo called the Glory.

The Glory is one of the most complicated bits of optics. It only forms when the cloud droplets are of uniform size: and that size must be just a few wavelengths of light (that's to say, just a few microns, or thousandths of a millimetre). The different colours cannot be explained completely in terms of normal named optical effects: refraction, reflection, interference. They can, however, be derived mathematically from James Clerk Maxwell's four equations of electromagnetism. If you feed those four equations – among the most elegant and satisfying in all physics – into a computer, it can calculate and display the Glory for any given size of cloud droplets. The computer can 'understand' Glories, but the human mind cannot!

If the cloud droplets are 20 microns wide, the inner red ring of the glory will be 5° across, which is roughly the length of your thumb when held at arms length. As the drops get smaller, the rings get bigger: droplets of 10 microns give an inner red ring of 8°, the length of your index finger.

A mountain riddle: what's the Brocken Spectre doing in the photo? Turn it round, and look at it the other way – the Spectre is taking a picture of the human. It's shooting straight into the sun, so the human's going to look a bit fuzzy.

There are seven nice ways up Blencathra: indeed, Sharp Edge and Halls Fell are among the nicest in all Lakeland.
On the other hand, in his *Pictorial Guide to the Northern Fells*, Wainwright gives a uniquely bad write-up to the four ravines that divide the southern face.

Blencathra seen from the Old Coach Road on the flank of Clough Head. The sheep seem to believe that they, rather than the mountain, are the subject of this photo... The picture does also serve as a sheep identifier, as the one on the left is Swaledale, those on the right are Herdwicks.

4. THE FOUR RAVINES

THE BAD WAYS UP BLENCATHRA?

BLEASE GILL · GATE GILL · BLENCATHRA: HALLS FELL · DODDICK GILL · SCALEY BECK · SCALES FELL · BANNERDALE CRAGS

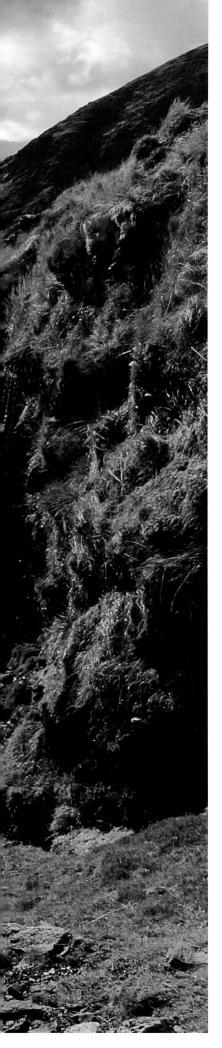

There are seven nice ways up: indeed, Sharp Edge and Halls Fell are among the nicest in all Lakeland. On the other hand, in his *Pictorial Guide to the Northern Fells*, Wainwright gives a uniquely bad write-up to the four ravines that divide the face of Blencathra. "There is nothing inviting in these shattered cliffs and petrified rivers of stone: the scene intimidates and repels." (I abridge slightly.) "Few who gaze upon these desolate walls are likely to feel any inclination and inspiration to scramble up through their arid, stony wildernesses to the contorted skyline so high above." That said, Wainwright himself went up here four times over: exploring each of the four streams that divide the face. And his descriptions are so unappealing that you can't read them without forming the strong desire to go up there to see if it's really so bad as he says.

SCALEY BECK

Here, says Wainwright, "there is little of interest". A sheep path tippy-toes through dwarf gorse, 20m above the stream and on its right (east) side. Once the stream has led you around various bends and right

OPPOSITE: The 'gulch' of Blease Gill, looking down towards Ullswater, Bleaberry Fell and Derwent Water. BELOW: Looking down into Scaley Beck, from Scales Fell.

into the heart of the hill, it stops. Above is a broad slope of heather with patches of scree. The scree is quite awkward to get up. But the heather is much worse. "There is little of interest" is a bit of Alfred Wainwright understatement. This is true heather hell. Right at the top things get pleasantly grassy, as a vague spur leads onto the Scales Fell ridgeline.

DODDICK GILL

Doddick Gill is even less pleasant than the preceding. "This is the roughest way of all. There is no comfort in it... For tough guys only, not to be used for descent. A route to commend heartily to one's worst enemy." I headed in hopefully. The sheep had eaten the vegetation of the lower gill into a new disposition, and the promised scrambling with hands on heather didn't take place. Neither, disappointingly, did the wetfoot continuation along the slabby bed of the stream.

Ahead, now, lies an "intimidating 1000ft facade of chaotic crags and scree". It's just as well Wainwright told me, as what I had in front of me was a high wall of mist. But the stream ran up into a mossy, black, and quite dramatic little ravine. A waterfall dripped in over the wall, and then turned sharp right and wafted uphill on the wind, spraying my back for the next twenty paces.

Up here I was supposed to climb the bilberry slope alongside. But it seemed simpler to stay in the ravine, so obtaining a very poor scramble Grade 1 – in the 800m of this ascent there are just 10m of scrambling. The first little pitch is on shattered wet rock, with plentiful incut holds, some of which are fairly firmly fixed on to the hill. Above that is a water-filled groove which can be avoided by a drier groove on the right. The dry groove is loose stones, moss and mud; accordingly I returned to the wet one, where wrist-deep flowing water meant no mud or moss, but in places quite good rock.

Above the ravine is steep grass with who knows what in the way of loose boulders and rotten rock in the mist all around. The stream becomes a scree groove, then disappears. I kept hopefully uphill, on little gravel ledges, to arrive on Halls Fell Ridge in the middle of its delightful upper section.

GATE GILL

Gate Gill is where the lead ore was – and some of it still is, so that the mines could conceivably reopen if lead gets more expensive. Before you're even on the mountain, immediately above Gategill Farm, the woods below the path hide a high dam, with a doorway in the bottom where the water escapes. This former reservoir has been used as a dump: here are

RIGHT: Looking down Doddick Gill.
BELOW: The top part of Doddick Gill.

GATE GILL

OPPOSITE and ABOVE: Entrance to Gate Gill. MIDDLE: The upper reservoir above Gategill farm; and one of its present-day contents. BOTTOM RIGHT: Waterfalls just above the Powder House. The old track leading to the mines is high on the left-hand slope.

souvenirs from the dawn of the aluminium age back in the 1950s.

At the fell wall, the path uses another old dam, a stone one this time. Just above is the powder house, where gunpowder was kept safely (well, fairly safely) away from the workings. A wide but little-walked path leads into a place of strange quartzy scree that's actually spoil heaps, interrupted by low stone walls. Two small holes lead into the hill; sinister streams trickle out of them, mineral-stained and chilled.

Above all the workings, a spurline between two streams gives the least steep way onwards and up. "Amidst the desolation of crag and scree... the green ribbon of Middle Tongue appears as an attractive oasis, providing the only grassy route to the summit escarpment. Its charms vanish when put to the test,

however, the lower part being rough and all of it tedious."

Wainwright is not wrong. The spur turns out to be heathery, with rocks under. Middle Tongue is certainly going to be unpleasant all the way. But uncertainty is so much more satisfying. So I tried to bypass some of it by following the right-hand (eastern) branch stream. The stream offers a grassy bank for a few metres, but then comes a crag. Here you scramble up the waterfall if you can, or else edge across the crag on heathery ledges, loose rock, and lumps of moss. Moss-climbing is a whole new skill, where you sink hands and feet into the squelch and hope to stay on by suction.

BELOW: Looking down Gate Gill. Once above the old mines in the lower gill, and the helpful path leading through them, this becomes one of the more arduous and less rewarding ways up or down Blencathra.

ABOVE AND FAR LEFT:
The hole to right of Gate
Gill stream is a drainage adit
for water escaping from the
mines upstream.
LEFT: Vein breccia, rock
shattered by movement along
a faultline, then cemented
together again by the quartz
which invaded the faultline
crack

BLEASE GILL

"Hard travelling over tough ground and wastes of scree make this no route for genteel walkers, but rough-necks will enjoy it," says Wainwright. In fact it starts off in a way that's almost attractive, with grassy stream banks leading into the hill. On either side, two of the nice ways up Blencathra, Blease Fell and Gategill Fell, lead up steeply and are soon inaccessible above walls of heather. In the bottom, the stream offers a few inches of grassy banking on one side or the other. Accordingly, I travelled ever inwards on one side or the other, leaping across the water 12 times to the crucial stream junction.

Now I could go up the stream on the left, or the spur in the middle. But Wainwright strongly advises the stream on the right. "The canyon is Wild West stuff – 'gulch' might be a better word."

AW's favourite form of cultural experience – possibly his only form of cultural experience – was going to the pictures to see films about cowboys. So to label this a place for the Lone Ranger and his Native American sidekick Tonto – Silver the pony would never cope with the scree – this is high praise. (Incidentally, in Spanish Tonto simply means 'stupid'. None of this Political Correctness nonsense in 1950s Hollywood. Not much of it in old AW either, of course.)

The gulch was indeed gulchy: scree floor with stream, rock walls not very high but atmospheric. Having started not unpleasantly, in fact, this route now turns into something exotic that's also altogether different from either Halls Fell or Sharp Edge. Beside the stream are loose stones, but also bright patches of moss and the occasional wild flower. Feeling romantic rather than ridiculous, Tonto rather than tonto, you cross the stream for the eighteenth time and emerge to the foot of a scree fan. There's no need to slog up the scree. Steep grass on the right leads up to one of my favourite Saddleback sites, the little green flattening called Knott Halloo, high on Gategill Fell and back in the previous chapter.

Just sometimes, the bad ways up can be the best ways of all.

OPPOSITE: Blease Gill, in a telephoto shot from High Rigg. The 'gulch' runs up to the right in the shadow area. Knott Halloo is sunlit on the right, just below the snowline. LEFT: Quartz veining in scree fragment near the top of Blease Gill (top). Sugar quartz, probably associated with a mineral vein. While the main mines were in Gate Gill, Blease Gill also contains one or two mine adits (middle). Woolly hair moss in Blease Gill (bottom).

Glenderaterra is the valley that's smaller than its own name – but just as nice. The name is British, starting with the Welsh 'glyn dwfr' that means glen of water, and finishing obscurely. The glen itself, somewhat similarly, peters out into the shapeless country behind Skiddaw and Blencathra. But on the way there, it cuts a dramatic and deep vee-slot, with trees and a little stream in its foot, and broken crags overhead. It is obviously akin to the Glenderamackin, at the other end of Blencathra; but otherwise it is mysteriously different from the cushion swells of this northern fell group.

A wide, well-made track contours half-way up the Blencathra side of the slot. It could have been designed just to show off this landscape feature (but actually it's one of the ways to Skiddaw House). A narrower one, incorporated into the Cumbria Way, does the same on the Skiddaw side. That path contours thrillingly below ever-steeper slopes of heather and rock. Below is the deep hollow of the beck, and ahead is a gradually widening, vee-shaped view of St John's Vale and the edge of Helvellyn. The slope gets steeper, until the path becomes a shelf hacked out of bare rock: and at this point (grid reference NY 294261) you turn the corner and the view reveals everything from Catbells to Clough Head, with the Vale of Keswick and Derwent Water. It almost tempts one to take up pipe-smoking, just so as to sit and smoke it at this particular path bend.

Seen from either of the two paths, the stream below seems too small to have carved this big valley. And yet the valley itself is not at all the classic U-shape of a glaciated one; it also lacks moraine hummocks. Glenderaterra: glacier-gouged, stream-slotted, or what?

The first thing to realise is that the valley was easier to carve than it looks. The largest and longest fault line in Lakeland starts here at the back of Skiddaw. Where two great land masses slide past one another, the rocks along the faultline are broken up and shattered; and this makes it relatively easy for the forces of erosion to carve out a valley. The fault that broke open the Glenderaterra continues south as the continuing valley line of St John's Vale and Dunmail Raise. It lies under the waters of both Grasmere and Elterwater, before finally defining the

line of Coniston Water: it is named for the last of these, as the Coniston Fault.

This large-scale faulting helped give us Glenderaterra. Even so, the stream itself is a 'misfit', not really big enough for the glen it lives in. There are two fairly plausible explanations. The glen might be a meltwater channel from the end of the last Ice Age. We know that big ice sheets came south out of Scotland. If these blocked off the end of Mosedale, the River Caldew could have formed a meltwater lake behind a great dirty grey ice mountain, its waters eventually draining out southwards to carve the gorge.

Less excitingly, the accepted theory is that the Glenderaterra is actually, what it doesn't look like, a hanging glacier valley. Screes falling from Lonscale Fell and Blencathra have filled in the U-curve of the original valley walls. As the final touch, the current Glenderaterra Beck has carved the very bottom to form the lowest notch of the vee-shape.

SKIDDAW FOREST: MORE TREES, PLEASE!

The places you get to if you go up Glenderaterra are not so great as the glen itself. The middle of this northern fell block has been worn down into a place of grassy tussocks, heather and bog. It's called 'Skiddaw Forest', but this is in the old sense of being a hunting preserve. Here are no trees apart from the scruffy plantation that shelters the old shepherd's dwelling, Skiddaw House. That plantation has been underplanted with native trees and will be better looking in a decade or two. Skiddaw House is, after a brief break in the early noughties, again a youth hostel. It may not be the most remote – the one at Black Sail in Ennerdale competes for that accolade – but Skiddaw House is certainly one of Britain's bleakest. And crossed on the track towards Skiddaw House is Roughton Gill, which as a route up Blencathra "holds no terrors at all... but most people will find it unexciting and dreary".

As with his description of the ravines on Blencathra's front, Wainwright's words almost compel us to try the Roughton Gill just to see whether we can be even slightly amused. The Roughton Gill beck heads uphill in a little green dell. After rain the stream is a splashy white, leaping up and down beside the walker like an over-enthusiastic little dog. The dell it does it in, is about to get a whole lot greener and more delvish. For Natural England has also noticed the anomaly of Skiddaw Forest being almost totally treeless. Its volunteers have, in 2008, planted thousands of small broadleaved trees in green plastic tubes all the way up Roughton Gill. They used specialist abseiling ecologists to position some of the downy birch, hazel and juniper.

On the track to Skiddaw House, looking back down Glenderaterra. A half-mile back this path divides. The main track is seen on the left-hand, Blencathra, flank of the valley: it eventually leads out and round to the Blencathra Centre above Threlkeld. On the right, behind and above the walkers, is the narrower path that contours out onto the southern slope of Lonscale Fell, eventually reaching Latrigg above Keswick. At the back of the picture is the gap of Dunmail Raise, defined by the same faultline as Glenderaterra.

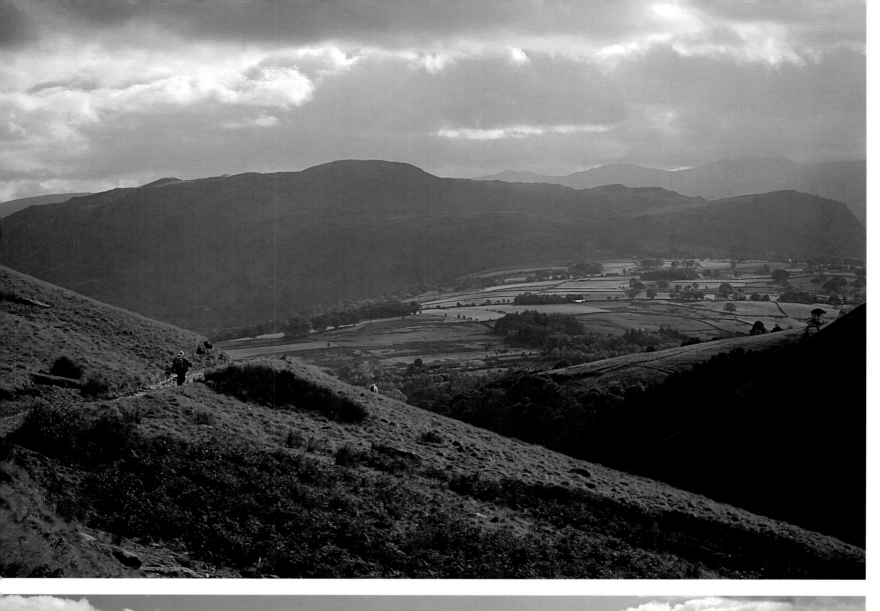

GLENDERATERRA

ABOVE: Glenderaterra, the deep V-gap between Skiddaw's Lonscale Fell (left) and Blease Fell of Blencathra. The contouring side-path to Latrigg is in sunlight on the far wall, below the broken ground. On the nearer side, the recently-improved path up Blease Fell curves upwards from the Blencathra Centre. The wide track to Skiddaw House is less obvious, contouring into Glenderaterra along the base of the hill ground. The foreground cairn is on Threlkeld Knotts.
TOP LEFT: Entering Glenderaterra on the track from the Blencathra Centre.
BOTTOM LEFT: From Great Calva, you look out through the gap of Glenderaterra and trace the faultline which formed it onwards, by Thirlmere and Dunmail Raise.

Above two middling-impressive waterfalls, the beck runs out on open hill. Now there is no more dell appeal, so you might as well turn right, up the grass slope towards the main ridge of Blencathra. And that grass slope has nothing to see but a whole lot more grass still to go up – while the wind gets windier and the rain gets colder. After a long time the gravelly ridgeline path appears and, just beyond it, the emptiness of the south face. Plus, if you're lucky and the cloud's up, that sudden view of half of Lakeland.

So Roughton Gill really is, as Wainwright already told us, not altogether exciting. Scenically even less impressive is the next one to the north, Sinen Gill. You cross it on the Skiddaw House track without really noticing – Roughton Gill, just before it, was the one that had the handsome clapperstone bridge. Sinen Gill is a trickle between banks of earth and shale, a break in the smooth grassland that's the western end of Blease Fell.

On a chilly spring morning I set off up Sinen Gill: and I was peering intently at those banks of shale, and into the bed of the stream. Almost at once I saw a strange-shaped stone: a stone that, among the shaly grey, was curved like the egg of a monstrous and mystic bird. And it was strangely coloured, as well. Off-white with black speckles might count as camouflage in some countries. But the monster bird made a mistake when it laid this one among the dark grey Skiddaw slates on the side of Blease Fell.

How many different reasons can there be for being on Blencathra? By the seventeenth ascent of this finest of Lakeland fells, it could be time to go geological. The Skiddaw Slate was described in the Introduction: it forms most of northern Lakeland. Skiddaw Slate, with all respect to its great age, is merely compressed mud. It breaks into little flat flakes to form lots of scree, and it becomes awkwardly slippery when wet. By the time you've been up Blencathra half a dozen times the Skiddaw Slate is familiar. But Skiddaw has also given its name to a second sort of stone – and the Skiddaw granite is more mysterious.

SKIDDAW SLATE HALF-BAKED
Back when Scotland was sliding in under the edge of England and all those rocks were being formed (the Devonian Era, if your memory goes back that far),

On the track just below Skiddaw House. The shallow stream groove immediately above the walkers is Sinen Gill; the deeper one behind is Roughton Gill, with the whole summit ridge of Blencathra above.

Looking down Roughton Gill and across Glenderaterra to the rocky slope of Lonscale Fell.

friction heat melted a blob of rock deep underground. That rock re-crystallised as the Skiddaw Granite, and Skiddaw may be the only mountain in Lakeland to have two different sorts of stone named after it. (The Coniston Limestone and the Coniston Grits are named for the village not the hill.) Since the Devonian Era the rocks have mostly been eroding, and the blob of granite is just starting to peep out. It can be seen in the bed of the Caldew, as well as in Sinen Gill on Blencathra.

The granite blob is roughly 3km long by 2km wide. The way we know the size of it is by measuring gravity. The granite is slightly lighter than other rocks, and the Earth's attraction above it is slightly less. Fell walking is a good way to lose weight: but fellwalking up Blencathra loses you that little bit extra. If you ascend Blencathra by its dull side round the back, the combined weight of you and your rucksack is reduced by almost 1gm.

When the granite blob arrived, it cooked and hardened the surrounding rocks. While Skiddaw slates are mostly not much good for climbing, Sharp Edge is slightly better than that; and this is because Sharp Edge is made of these stones rebaked by the arrival of the granite.

Geologists call the effect a 'metamorphic areole'. Metamorphic means changed by getting heated afterwards. You'll have to look up areole yourself, as this is a respectable fellwalking book where we don't discuss naked ladies (apart perhaps from the Maid of Buttermere).

It's disappointing that the actual granite is almost covered up. But geologists get excited just by a glimpse of the areole. Yes, it's not unlike those top-shelf magazines of the 1950s. All the stuff that matters is covered in severe grey slate or, at best, by a tantalisingly lacy film of glacier debris – so then a mere glimpse of the areole is incredibly exciting... On this (rather forced) analogy, the Zoo and Nuts magazines of today are like rocks crassly displayed in a quarry rather than lichen-covered or stream washed on a real mountainside.

But by the time you reach the foot of Sinen Gill, you've already missed half the fun. (For the purposes of the present section, it will be assumed that geology is fun.) Start again from the Blencathra Centre, and this time keep only one eye on Lonscale Fell and the Glenderaterra, reserving the other, the intellectual eye, for the rocks and stones under your feet.

Ordinary Skiddaw slate can be looked at in the small quarry that constitutes the car park. That slate is grey, fairly brittle, and – unsurprisingly – slaty; it breaks away in thin bits.

Half a mile later, as the track curves into the

Skiddaw slate in a Mungrisdale quarry (Top). Chiastolite slate, weathered with lichen, Bakestall (Middle). Cordierite crystals in hornfels (heat-altered slate), displayed on a fresh unweathered stone block beside the Skiddaw House track at its crossing of Glenderaterra Beck (Bottom).

beginning of Glenderaterra, the rock has altered. It is heavier, denser, darker, and less slaty: it is on its way to becoming the heat-altered rock called 'hornfels'. If the sun is shining from the correct direction, you might detect in a small roadside cutting a faint sparkle from the mineral mica. This mica sparkle is obvious to geologists, invisible to the rest of us, who learn that 'very well displayed' in a geological guide actually means 'can't see it'. The expression we need is 'very striking exposure' – which means 'visible even to an amateur who didn't even bring his hand lens because he hasn't got one'.

And at the very next gill there is just such a 'very striking exposure'. The gill is an unnamed one down the flank of Blease Fell (grid reference NY 299269). Its stream runs across the track, with a small waterfall

just above. The washed out banking has slaty stones which carry marks like bits of broken old grass stalks, yellowish white and about 2cm long. They could be fossils, but they are not. They are crystals of a mineral called chiastolite. Chiastolite is an aluminium silicate, which makes it, chemically speaking, about as ordinary as you can get in the earth's crust. What makes it odd are the little black dots in the centre of each rod-shaped crystal: these are inclusions of graphite.

According to the lore of crystal healing, chiastolite promotes problem solving and aids change. Oddly, the geologists agree completely… For, further along the track you reach the stone-slab bridge over Roughton Gill. Here the little pale rods of chiastolite are much less common, and instead the rock has

slightly projecting black spots up to 1cm wide. These are a new mineral called cordierite. It is a slightly more complex aluminium silicate, involving also iron or magnesium. Its presence shows that we are getting closer to the underground lump of granite – in terms of the children's game hide-and-seek, we are getting 'warmer'. Water incorporated in the original slaty rocks was being driven out by the heat of the granite lump. At geological temperatures and pressures water, as superheated steam, is a lively chemical, able to create and then eliminate these interesting crystals.

In another 50 metres, at the crossing of Glenderaterra Beck, you might see a reclining geologist; a geologist facing away from that fine vee-notch view of the high valley and central Lakeland,

ABOVE: Bakestall, looking across the Solway Firth to Scotland. The stones around this cairn have chiastolite crystals, showing the close-up photo. These slim crystals can be seen in stones underfoot across a wide swathe of the Skiddaw massif, and in the summit cairns of Lonscale Fell and of Skiddaw itself.
TOP LEFT: Looking down Sinen Gill across Glenderaterra to Lonscale Fell.
BOTTOM LEFT: Skiddaw Granite in Sinen Gill.

to take pictures of a pair of nondescript grey boulders below the track. The boulders are interesting. They are no longer even slightly slaty, but have been altered to smooth dark-grey hornfels. The cordierite shows as small black specks like shrivelled ants. These Skiddaw Slates have been snuggling up right against the red-hot granite magma; the Skiddaw Granite itself is only a few meters away, just underneath the ground.

And sure enough, as you head up the Sinen Gill stream, there comes a small waterfall just like somewhere on Dartmoor, or a corner of the Cairngorms, or anywhere else not in the Lake District where water falls over great square chunks of granite. The granite is white, and speckly, and rounded at its edges; and there's another 10 or 20 cubic kilometres of it just under the ground. Amazing!

Having found the granite, the next thing to look for is its edge. Rocks don't fade into one another in the way that heather fades into grass and then, as you go on up the hill, to scree and mossy bits. Rocks change between one footfall and the next: in a single stride, you might cross 50 million years or more. Upstream from the small waterfall by 50 metres, on the undercut northern bank, you can see the join. What makes it quite obvious is the way it's only two miles from the Blencathra Field Centre, and accordingly geologists have been scrabbling like rabbits to expose the rock join. Above: the pitted grey hornfels; two inches further down, the pale granite. Span one million lifetimes between thumb and forefinger...

So if the seventeenth time up Blencathra was the one to go geologically, it has now considered Glenderaterra, and how it got there: and used crystal-gazing to track down the Skiddaw Granite. The final question: what will be the excuse for the eighteenth ascent? And that one won't be hard. There's always another reason for being on this best of fells, Blencathra.

LEFT: Seen in section across the rods, each chiastolite crystal has a black, graphite centre. The crystals are up to 3cm long.
OPPOSITE: Waterfall above Skiddaw House track in Glenderaterra: this gill cuts into chiastolite slate.

FOLLOWING PAGES: Looking out through the slot of Glenderaterra to Derwent Water and Scafell Pike: view from Mungrisdale Common above Sinen Gill.

To the east and north of Saddleback there is a continuation of several hills of less note, principally covered with heath and disagreeable to the eye, which are terminated in the open cultivated part of the country. The most remarkable of these are Souther-fell, Bowscale-fell, Carrock-fell and Caldbeck fells.

A Topographical Description of Cumberland, Westmoreland, etc –
John Housman 1800

Caldbeck and Caldbeck Fells
Are worth all England else
– Anon

It's extremely easy to disprove that rhyme about the Caldbeck Fells. You don't need a dreary day to do it, though a dreary day does help. Leave aside that it's a rhyme that doesn't rhyme – the Caldbeck Fells are gently sloping grass, and flat bits. The grass is brown, and the flat bits are bog. While all Lakeland is lovely, here, if anywhere, is the area slightly less lovely than all the rest. No rocks emerge, no screes and gullies. The only excitement you'll get is when you're confronted with a fence, or even meet a sheep. When you do meet a sheep, tell it a joke. It might smile, and then you can see its teeth.

"There is a tradition here that, for ages, the *copper*, with which the mountains are said to abound, affects the waters of the brooks, which are supposed to have issued through the veins of that ore, to such a degree, as to tinge the teeth of the sheep of a gold-colour," recorded William Hutchinson in 1794 – but admitted that he didn't even believe it himself.

The very names here – with just one exception – are unexciting. No Seat Sandal, no Grike, no John Bell's Banner: instead we find Brae Fell (meaning 'Hill Hill') and Meal Fell (meaning 'Hump Hill'). Or else we don't find Brae Fell and Meal Fell: they barely rise above the general grassland, and in mist they scarcely exist. The high point hereabouts is unoriginally named as High Pike, of which the first part is more or less correct: 658m is reasonably high. But 'Pike' implies spikiness, where High Pike is a damp plateau. One group of people who didn't enjoy the Caldbeck Fells at all were the four escaped German POWs loose in the area in 1944. After four days on the fell they were lucky enough to run into PC Robert Thompson on a routine patrol (presumably on his bike) and gratefully invited him to recapture them.

The non-rhyming rhyme isn't, however, celebrating

the bogs or the fences. It isn't even celebrating how good it is to ride horses across here while killing foxes with the aid of dogs – though according to John Peel of Caldbeck and the famous song about him, the fox-killing here is first rate. The rhyme celebrates not so much the fells as what's inside them. The couplet is Cumbrian, and as such is coolly practical. Scafell Pike is just 'watter and stanes', useless even to a sheep. High Pike, on the other hand, is cold cash.

HIGH PIKE INSIDE OUT

I toured High Pike under the guidance of Ian Tyler, proprietor of the Keswick Mining Museum and a man who, quite literally, knows these hills inside out. A soggy September day served to bring out to the full the faint attractions – in fellwalking terms – of the Caldbeck Fells. Damp brown grass faded after a few metres into grey mist.

The first interesting place is an area of bare gravel near Carrock Beck. It looks like some scree but it was once a fulling mill, with water-powered machinery for combing wool and hammering it into felts. After 1500 this was adapted as smelt mill, melting lead out of the ores carried down from higher up the hill. These early miners were only interested in lead, so whitish barites and blue-green copper minerals were left lying around in the spoil among the rounded lumpy stuff that's half-melted lead ore. The nearby stream washes out fragments of the miners' clay pipes.

This particular smelt mill is 16th century, one of the earliest. Driggeth Mine, uphill from here, yielded both lead and, later, copper. Lead has been important since Roman times for making water pipes and covering roofs. An early use of copper was for sheathing ships bottoms: Columbus' three ships were copper-bottomed.

The lower part of the Driggeth mine complex was worked right into the 1960s. Flat places on the fellside were a dressing floor and the settling ponds. A few old black timbers are the remains of a jig, a wooden trough; ore was crushed to a standard size (such as half an inch) and jiggled in the jig. Heaver, more valuable, ore ended up at the bottom. Further down the hill, another round flat place housed an 18-foot wide buddle, a device like an upside down Japanese umbrella. When it span round, the lighter stones moved up to the edges while the heavier ore remained down in the centre. Somewhat similarly today, a centrifuge, a huge spinning cylinder, is used to separate Uranium 238 from its chemically-identical U235 for nuclear reactors and bombs. The slightly lighter U235 drifts to the outside. Thus, smuggling centrifuges into Iran gets you a very long prison sentence.

Little Calva and Great Calva, from Bakestall.

Around the hill shoulder in Drygill Beck, the drainage adit is still doing its job, with a healthy small stream emerging from the hole in the hill. The tunnel was hand-hewn with picks, which you can tell because it lacks the holes for explosives seen in more recent shafts. After 50 metres it becomes dry, but then rises to a collapsed section.

Above the adit, we move into the main mining area, with strangely white and knobby screes which are actually spoil heaps. Here is one rare mineral, called campylite, which looks like bright yellow chickenpox. A hand-sized specimen, with good crystals, is worth thousands of pounds – even though it's nothing but a slightly different sort of lead ore. The old miners would simply have thrown it into the pot with the rest. It's valuable because it looks really weird, but more because it's found only on High Pike and at one locality in Sweden. What adventures they had, those Victorian mineral collectors, up into the remote desert wilderness of Caldbeck!

To collect minerals anywhere in the Caldbeck Fells you need a permit from the National Park, which manages the sites. So here's something new and unusual by way of a life of crime: unlicensed collectors running the gauntlet of the national park rangers. Two such adventurers have been caught in ceiling collapses, one having to be extracted by the Mountain Rescue. The other got lucky when the collapsing rocks hit the end of the plank and catapulted him upwards, so that he ended wedged across the top of the cavern as the rubble piled up below.

Some of these criminal collectors are in it for the money, even damaging archaeological sites with heavy equipment. Rather more are after the fun of finding out what's underground, while dodging the rangers. Mines of Lakeland Exploration Society, or MOLES, the organisation Ian Tyler helped to set up, does its exploration responsibly, in consultation with archeologists, with insurance and proper safety precautions. Have they ever lost a member? "No; not even anybody seriously maimed," said Ian. "Just a few superficial scars…"

We head up over loose stones to the top of the workings. "Now this is really interesting," says IanTyler. "What you're standing on here is one massive dump."

In the mist on the summit of High Pike, a fellow mines-explorer passed on some High Pike gossip. A famous mountaineer and a very famous older mountaineer recently walked over High Pike with two children; their intention a crossing of Blencathra down to Threlkeld. But, in the mist, they overshot the summit of High Pike.

"You've got the map, have you?" says the younger famous mountaineer.

"No," says the older and even more famous mountaineer, "I haven't got the map. I thought you would have the map." The children, out with two famous mountaineers, certainly weren't carrying a map.

At this point appears out of the mist an elderly woman fellwalker, fully equipped in Gore-tex, walking poles and all.

"Are you going to say it?" asks the more famous mountaineer. "'Cos I'm not blooming asking her if we can look at her map…"

This story is gossip, so I shall not name either of the mountaineers allegedly involved.

Sandbed Mines are at the back of High Pike, though it all joins up underground. Gravelly pits across the hillside mark the line of the vein. Here are blue linarite (a combined lead-copper mineral), and

TOP: Upper part of Driggeth Mine, High Pike.
ABOVE LEFT: Remains of jig, Driggeth Mine.
ABOVE RIGHT: Turquoise-coloured copper minerals and blue-grey sphalerite, a zinc ore.

dirty green pyromorphite (a lead mineral involving chlorine). A deep grassy hollow with one rocky side is Number One Engine Shaft, which is 400 feet deep. According to Ian Tyler: "Some of the finest timbering in Lakeland is buried under there – shafts that run out half a mile either way, through rotten rock."

Further down are the foundations of the mine manager's office, and his garden. It's not easy to imagine this bare hillside of brown gravel as a place of busy industry. And it's even harder to conjure up mentally, on the misted hill, the mine manager's hollyhocks and roses. The mist rises just enough to let us see and sneer at the single wind turbine just outside the national park boundary above Hesket Newmarket. Old mines, though: there's nothing intrusive or unsightly about them.

CALDBECK AND HESKET

The hill-foot villages of Caldbeck and Hesket Newmarket are a lost corner beyond the highways of the M6 and A66. But in the mining times, and before, they were big and busy. Caldbeck lay on the main road to Carlisle. A hostelry here was founded by the Priory of Carlisle so long ago that it was dissolved under King John early in the 13th century.

The road through Caldbeck was used by the Wordsworths heading for Scotland in 1803. Below

TOP LEFT: Pattinson's Level, at Drygill.
TOP RIGHT: Spoil heap at Driggeth Mine, with campylite on the front of the main quartz stone centre bottom, and traces of greenish pyromorphite at bottom right.
RIGHT: Pyromorphite, on a stone about 12cm wide, at Sandbed Mine; and campylite (bottom right) at Drygill, on a black background of manganese ore and soot.

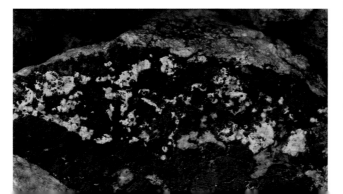

BACK O' SKIDDAW

OPPOSITE: First sunlight on Knott, seen from Bowscale Tarn.(Top). Great Calva from the north, the ridgeline connecting it with the rest of the Caldbeck Fells (left). Swinside farm, in Mosedale (right).
TOP: On Brae Fell, heading down northwards towards Fell Side (left). Looking up Mosedale towards Skiddaw (Right).
MIDDLE: Great Calva and Knott from Mungrisdale Common. BOTTOM: Roughton Gill and Knott from the north.

TOP LEFT: Millstone for grinding ore, from Roughton Gill mines, now in St Kentigern's churchyard, Caldbeck.
TOP RIGHT: The Howk, in 1797, from Hutchinson's History of Cumberland. Book illustration by courtesy of Carlisle Library.
LEFT: Above the Howk, Caldbeck.

the village, the little limestone nook called the Howk was an industrial estate, the River Caldew being harnessed for papermaking, wool processing, and bobbin making.

Coleridge visited the Howk in October 1800, on the same day as his ascent of Carrock Fell described below. He was back three years later, but his notebook of 1800 gives his fresh, first impression.

"On the bank of the beck prodigious quantities of that huge-leafed plant (burdock). Before you, stand fairies' parlours and fine cathedral seats overhung by the rock… Go again into the cavern and see another chamber, crawl into it. At the end one round hole through which I glimpse another waterfall. Shut my eyes: the noise of water like that when you are in a mill, a room off the great wheel. Climb out through the window hole… Rocks overhanging from a big square pillar three yards at least. Great swinging pendula of ivy almost down to the water. The inclined rocks make an inclined bridge over the beck."

Today, a health-and-safety fence blocks the ledge leading to the fairy parlour. But sound common sense has made the fence a stout one, so as not to injure or inconvenience those visitors who may wish to clamber over it.

Not that those visitors are many. The fells have replaced the fairies' grotto in the affection of Lakeland visitors; mineral-hunting is today a minor sort of sport. Caldbeck remains a handsome limestone village, its car park tucked out of sight at the riverside. Mary Robinson, the Maid of Buttermere, moved here on her second, non-bigamous, marriage and is buried in Caldbeck churchyard. But the more famous former resident was the all-time fan of a sport soon to become even less mainstream than mineral-hunting.

UNPLEASANT MR PEEL

Did ye ken John Peel wie his cwote seay gray,
Did ye ken John Peel at the breck o' day;
Did ye ken John Peel gang far, far away,
Wid his hounds an' his horn in a mwornin?

John Peel lived from 1776 to 1854 in Caldbeck, and only in Caldbeck. Versions of his song mentioning Troutbeck are just wrong. The latterday Blencathra Hunt follows its hounds on foot, but Peel hunted the

The Howk, and (below) some of its spring flowers, kingcup, wood anemone, and celandine.

Caldbeck fells on his white (or in horsemen's terms, 'grey') fell pony. One of his descendents described him to Harry Griffin as "ter'ble lang in th' leg and lish, wi' a fine, girt neb, and grey eyes that could see for ever". ('Lish' is supple or sprightly, 'neb' is nose.) He once hunted over 70 miles in a single day in 1829. His 'cwote seay gray'– not 'gay', that's another outsiders' error – was of the Skiddaw cloth, made of undyed wool interwoven from the younger, darker-coloured Herdwick sheep and the older, white-coloured ones.

Peel spoke such broad Cumbrian that even his own nephew had trouble understanding him. "When he wasn't huntin, he was aye drinkin'," his nephew Robert told the local historian AG Bradley. The song was written by his friend Woodcock Graves, owner of the Howk's bobbin mill, and the 'Oddfellow' after whom the village pub is named. The song was tossed off one snowy, drunken, evening in 1824, to an old tune. The current tune was attached around 1870; the original tune 'Bonnie Annie' is described by Harry Griffin as 'rather dreary'. "By Jove, Peel," said Woodcock, "you'll be sung when we're both run to earth."

"Why make a hero of one who neglected his farm and impoverished his family by his unrestrained pursuit of hunting?" asked the Rector of Carlisle, very pertinently, in 1929. Even according to his friend John Woodcock Graves, "business of any shape was utterly neglected…indeed this neglect extended to paternal duties of his family. I believe he would not have left the drag of a fox on the impending death of a child or any other earthly event." By the end of his life, Peel's neglect brought his family into serious debt – only paid off through gifts from his friends. He died on November 13, 1854, aged 78, probably after a fall while hunting.

By the 1880s, foxes in the fells had been hunted almost to extinction. In the 20th century, numbers rose again after the low country around the fells was deliberately restocked by hunts.

Two of Peel's whips, a battered hunting horn, and the coat "so grey" are now held at Tullie House Museum in Carlisle.

BELOW: Caldbeck Fells, from Dale Beck just upstream from the Howk. Carrock Fell just visible left, with Roughton Gill at centre.

In 2009 the Caldbeck transmission mast was being rebuilt as part of the switchover to digital TV. The slightly higher new tower, at 337m or 1106ft, is the third tallest structure in the British Isles. The UK's 16 tallest structures are all communications masts. The Caldbeck mast is one and a half times the height of Canary Wharf. Its base is at 290m, so if it was earth and stones all the way up it would be Lakeland's 124th highest summit, just after Yewbarrow, and only 30m lower than Carrock Fell. Its line of red lights makes it a useful beacon for night walkers on the northern fells.

CALDEBECK

TOP: Church of St Kentigern (or Mungo).
MIDDLE and BOTTOM LEFT: Dusk countryside beside Dale Beck upstream from the Howk.
BOTTOM RIGHT: The Oddfellows Arms was named for John Peel's songwriting crony Woodcock Graves, and contains his portrait and other items of local history up to and including an account of the new Caldbeck TV tower.
OPPOSITE: John Peel's horn and hound are shown on his gravestone (top).
The house where Woodcock Graves composed 'D' ye ken John Peel', complete with foxy knocker (middle left).
Caldbeck village pond (right).
BOTTOM: House dating from 1666 opposite the Oddfellow's Arms (left).
Church of St Kentigern (or Mungo). The lamplit steps lead down to Mungo's well, a spring at the riverside used for baptisms by the saint and right through to today. The church and the Medieval packhorse bridge have been built beside it (right).

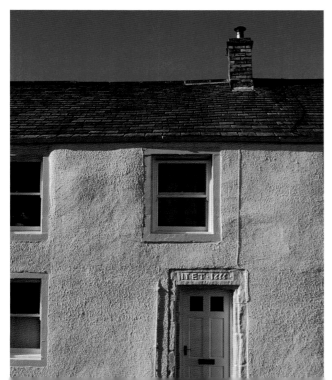

Gentle souls, connoisseurs of bog cotton and fence wire, should stay clear of Carrock Fell. Carrock is the Back o' Skiddaw's non-squelchy one. It rises in crag, scree and boulderfield, just to remind the rest of the Back o' Skiddaw that this is still Lakeland really.

Carrock Fell from Hutton Roof

7. CARROCK FELL

THIRSTY WORK AT THE BACK OF SKIDDAW

CLOUGH HEAD SOUTHER FELL BOWSCALE FELL CARROCK FELL HIGH PIKE

Black, coarse-stoned, rough-windowed houses; some with outer staircases, like Swiss houses; a sinuous and stony gutter winding up hill and round the corner, by way of street. Old Carrock gloomed down upon it all in a very ill-tempered state; and rain was beginning.
– Charles Dickens in Hesket Newmarket with Wilkie Collins, Sept 1857 (from *The Lazy Tour of Two Idle Apprentices*)

The Old Crown pub at Hesket Newmarket has devised a challenge walk to help its regulars work up a thirst for its village-brewed ale. The 18-mile Old Crown Round takes in four of the nearby fells. Skiddaw and Saddleback are fine hills in anybody's book; Great Cockup is grassy but has Lakeland's most entertaining name. The final hill is Carrock Fell.

The thirsty fellwalkers of Hesket Newmarket like this hill so much, they've named their beer after it. Carrock Fell is heather-coloured, delicious but requires a strong head – and the beer is the same, but is also described as 'beguilingly smooth' (the hill, on the other hand, is beguilingly rough). The other three fells of the Old Crown Round can also be taken in liquid form: four tasty half-pints of Skiddaw, Blencathra Bitter, Old Carrock and Great Cockup make an altogether more tempting project than 18 miles of tough hill, not to mention a paddle in the Caldew.

In an exciting development for hardwalking drinkers, in 2009 the Old Crown brewed a fifth of the northern fells, High Pike – described as 'a full nutty malt complemented by a complex bitterness'. Accordingly, the Old Crown Round increases to 22 miles with about 8000ft of ascent. The beer-themed fellbagger might also mount 'Catbells Pale Ale', 'Haystacks', and 'Helvellyn Gold' – but not perhaps 'Old Doris', the landlady's mother.

Mountain marathons name their routes as E (for elite), A, B, C and D. The Saunders Lakeland Mountain Marathon is more original. Its courses are named after worthwhile fells of various sizes. There's the Scafell (for top-class fellrunning navigators); the Bowfell, the Kirkfell, the Wansfell (for walkers in boots) – and the Carrock Fell. Carrock class is for reasonably experienced runners.

Some people like the Back o' Skiddaw for its own sake. After the boot-ripping rigours of Bow Fell and Great Gable, the scariness of Striding Edge and Steeple, they want some flat ridges and gentle yellow

OPPOSITE: Looking down the River Caldew to Carrock Fell; view from Skiddaw House

grasses. They like to feel their feet sink into something squelchy, and the cool peaty waters flowing slowly into their socks. They appreciate the solitude – a solitude that's down to the way that most of us think the Back o' Skiddaw is a bit of a bore.

Those gentle souls, those connoisseurs of bog cotton and fence wire, should stay clear of Carrock Fell. Carrock is the Back o' Skiddaw's non-squelchy one. It rises in crag, scree and boulderfield, just to remind the rest of the Back o' Skiddaw that this really is still Lakeland. Coleridge, who loved every sort of Lakeland scenery, appreciated Carrock Fell, which was at the limit of a long daywalk from his Keswick base. He climbed it first on 11 October 1800, in his first Lakeland autumn.

On this mountain Carrock, at the summit of which are the remains of a vast Druid Circle of Stones, I was wandering –; when a thick cloud came on, and wrapped me in such Darkness that I could not see ten yards before me – and with the cloud a storm of Wind & Hail, the like of which I had never before seen & felt. At the very summit is a cone of Stones, built by the Shepherds, and called the Carrock Man.... At the bottom of the Carrock Man I seated myself for shelter, but the winds became so fearful & tyrannous, that I was apprehensive, some of the stones might topple down upon me, so I groped my way farther down and came to 3 rocks... each one supported by the other like a Child's House of Cards, & in the Hollow & Screen which they made I sate for a long while sheltered, as if I had been in my own Study in which I am now writing – Here I sate, with a total feeling worshipping the power & 'eternal Link' of Energy. The Darkness vanished, as by enchantment – : far off, far far off, to the South the mountains of Glaramara & Great Gavel [Great Gable], and their Family, appeared distinct, in deepest, sablest *Blue*. I rose, & behind me was a rainbow bright as the brightest.

I descended by the side of a torrent, and passed, or rather crawled (for I was forced to descend on all fours), by many a naked waterfall, till, fatigued and hungry (and with a finger almost broken, and which [7 days later] remains swelled to the size of two fingers), I reached the narrow vale, and the single house nestled in ash and sycamores. [According to his notebooks, this was a direct descent south to Swinside.]

(Letter to Humphrey Davy, 18th Oct 1800)

He begged milk and sour bread from a house with 'dirt and every appearance of misery', but even so was not permitted to pay for his food, except if he could offer any recipe for the rheumatics. This he was in a position to obtain for his hostess from the top chemist of the time, his friend Humphrey Davy.

Charles Dickens and Wilkie Collins also made the ascent; Collins, as the leading horror novelist of the 1850s, presumably revelling in the weather even though it was slightly less nasty than it had been for Coleridge 57 years before.

The wind, a wind unknown in the happy valley, blows keen and strong; the rain-mist gets impenetrable; a dreary little cairn of stones appears. [Wilkie Collins], drenched and panting, stands up with his back to the wind, ascertains distinctly that this is the top at last, looks round with all the little curiosity that is left in him, and gets, in return, a magnificent view of – Nothing!

(*Idle Tour of Two Lazy Apprentices* Charles Dickens 1857)

On the descent Dickens broke the compass. Then Wilkie Collins fell over a small cliff and sprained his ankle. Dickens carried his friend off the hill, delighted at the way he was re-enacting a scene from a melodrama of Arctic exploration, *The Frozen Deep*, which the two of them had composed and performed the previous year.

CARROCK AND CUILLIN

So is Carrock Fell the Beast of the Back o' Skiddaw? Well, this hill is certainly working hard on its image in this respect, even stealing its clothing from the mountains of Skye. Sgurr nan Gillean – Sgurr Alasdair – the Inaccessible Pinnacle and the Bhasteir Tooth: these are Britain's finest and fiercest. And their black gabbro rock – trouser-ripping rough, but superbly grippy to climb or scramble – is also the rock of Carrock. Its only UK outcrops are on the isles of Skye and Rhum, and here on Carrock Fell. (Well actually, there's another tiny bit of it at the very top of Hindscarth, above Newlands.)

Carrock's gabbro is about 10 times as old as Skye,

Summit cairn on Carrock Fell: Blencathra beyond.

and less lively and vigorous in its expression. It's middling grey rather than satanic black. And gabbro-grabbers who come expecting England's answer to Sgurr Alasdair may find that the fell isn't quite all it's Carrocked up to be. The gabbro is only a narrow belt of crag above Stone Ends. And really it's just as well the English gabbro is so scarce and scrappy. Gabbro climbing makes even the Borrowdale Volcanic of Scafell and Pillar Rock seem ordinary.

Above the gabbro bits, Carrock Fell's summit is a boulderfield of pink granite. Northwards from the summit lies greenish diorite. All three rocks are formed deep underground from big lumps of cooling magma. Big lumps of underground magma tend to boil minerals out of the surrounding rocks, and those minerals then condense in cracks higher up. Immediately around Carrock Fell are the remains of mines for tungsten, lead, arsenic and iron, and a silver mine going back to Elizabethan times.

As well as stones stolen from the Isle of Skye, Carrock has another non-Lakeland feature. On its summit is a hill fort, about five acres (two hectares) in size. The most visible remains of its former stone walls are just below the summit on the south side.

Oddly, this is almost the only one in Lakeland. Counties with far fewer hills have far more in the way of hill forts. Somerset has a hill fort every five miles. But then, any sensible Iron-Ager living in Wasdale wouldn't retreat behind prepared walls when he could retreat into Netherbeck or Hollow Stones. In the same way, the mountainous island of Crete does not have, and has never needed, fortified hill villages. And presumably it's only because Carrock Fell's right at the edge that they thought of it for a fort.

We know just as little about the Iron Age people who built this fort as we do of the Bronze-Agers who came before them and made the stone circle at Castlerigg on the other side of Blencathra. To work iron you need a more efficient furnace, able to reach white-heat rather than the mere red-heat required for copper, tin or bronze. Iron makes a stronger and sharper spear, and the Iron Age people quickly took over the country; the Romans record them as fierce opponents.

Today, archeologists are slowly discovering the softer side of life in the Iron Age. Excavations elsewhere suggest that within Carrock's hill fort there may have been a village of round huts, made of willow-twig coated with mud and cowpats. Some recent researchers claim that the orientation of the openings has a spiritual significance, with the light flowing across the floor in feng shui patterns. They wove tartan cloth which they pinned with broaches of copper. Roman historians tell us of their religious professionals, the druids.

Wealthy and sophisticated Iron-Agers made collections of interesting art objects. Mind you, it may be a mistake to consider them as totally in touch with their feminine sides – those interesting art objects were swords.

ONTO CALDBECK FELLS

Old mine tracks give easy access to High Pike from various directions. From Hesket Newmarket the grassy Cumbria Way ascends gradually by Nether Row and Potts Gill Mine. From Mosedale, the Cumbria Way's other end is a stony track which passes the wooden shelter hut at Great Lingy Hill. The wooden sleeping platform of this is quite comfortable, but the thin wooden walls don't provide much warmth, and you must carry in water. The situation is a fine one.

From Calebreck to the east, similar tracks pass different mines: one by Carrock Beck and Driggeth, another by How Beck and Sandbed Mine. Longer, rougher moorland routes arrive over Great Sca Fell or up Roughton Gill. Or from Dash Beck, a small path leads up through the heather onto Little Calva. Indeed, these rough grassy slopes are tiresome in parts but nowhere do they seriously obstruct the walker. Only routes onto Carrock Fell provide serious challenge. The most direct is a narrow path from Mosedale, zigzagging up the southeastern flank. Coming down this in the dark, I have had my ankles savaged by small gorse bushes. A more recently formed path takes the steep stony spur directly above the village.

To examine the gabbro outcrops of Carrock Fell, start from Stone Ends Farm. Roadside rocks provide gabbro bouldering, fierce rock climbs a few metres in length. A path slants up and left below the gabbro crags of Stone Ends, with one steep eroded scree section. Once past the crags, go up the steep green gully of Further Gill. As the slope eases, keep straight up, or else take a heather path that contours out to the right, and crosses along the top of Stone End crags. This path is narrow and exposed, with views right down to Stone Ends Farm.

Another interesting line heads up Mosedale to the traces of old Carrock Mine. Turn right, up Brandy Gill. Near the foot, a small rocky gorge ends at a small waterfall, easily climbed with your right hand and foot in the water. Or the gorge can be avoided on the right. At about 500m altitude, note the small abandoned adit beside another small waterfall.

*Bowscale Fell, Blencathra's Atkinson Pike,
and River Caldew, from Carrock Fell.
The shaded hollow at centre holds
Bowscale Tarn.*

CARROCK FELL

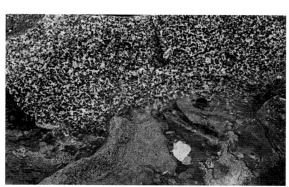

OPPOSITE: Collapsed Iron Age stonework on Carrock Fell summit; view to Vale of Eden
BOTTOM: Carrock Fell from Bannerdale Crags; Mosedale runs out to the Vale of Eden and the distant Pennines.
THIS PAGE (FAR LEFT): Blockfield of slightly pinkish granite at Carrock summit.
THIS PAGE (LEFT): More odd rocks of the Eycott Volcanics, diorite and granophyre, at Sandbed Mines (above); gabbro and parsley fern, lower down the hill, above Stone Ends.

ABOVE: Site of Carrock Mine, looking down Mosedale. After having closed and reopened half a dozen times depending on the strategic need for tungsten, the mine's buildings have now been cleared away. Some rubble remains here at the old mill site.

BELOW: Dug out vein called Harding Vein North, alongside Brandy Gill.

CARROCK FELL MINE

The Brandy Gill mine yielded lead and copper back in the 18th century. But the mining was difficult, because of a useless and very tough black ore, which was actually that of the metal tungsten. Even if anyone had a use for it, that metal was almost impossible to smelt out because of its extremely high melting point. Around the turn of the 19th century, it was realised that tungsten (in German, wolfram) because of that high melting point, was ideal for filaments of electric light bulbs. It was far longer lasting than carbonised bamboo, the previous best.

This was so exciting that in 1895 an electric railway was to be built linking Caldbeck with Wigton northwards, and southwards with Greystoke, Troutbeck, and the Penrith-Keswick railway. Mining for metals requires a special combination of qualities: boundless hope in the face of discouragement, and also very strong arms and legs. The railway, needless to say, didn't happen.

Around 1905 it was discovered that a small addition of tungsten can greatly harden steel plate. This is extremely useful for armour plating, supposing anybody was intending to go to war... A small group of Germans bought up the mine: some historians suspect that their funding came from the German government. At any rate, they shared the traditional view of the Caldbeck Fells. "This wolfram is *wunderschön* (wonderful). Much better than your famous Lakeland scenery!"

By 1907 the mine at the foot of Brandy Gill employed 105 workers and had penetrated 97 yards into the hill. The ore was coming out at 2 per cent tungsten concentrate, a remarkably rich and pure source of the metal. In 1913 the mine was as productive as ever; but the world tungsten price plunged, the Germans went bankrupt, and the mine closed.

In 1914, with Caldbeck tungsten now incorporated into the German High Seas Fleet, World War One broke out; and the Carrock Fell Mine reopened. A new mill was built. Up-to-date and very noisy drills powered by compressed air replaced the old hand tools. The most modern of waterwheels were assembled to power the crushing mills and jigs. The climber and photographer George Abraham, in his role as reporter for Autocar magazine, was invited into the workings. He described the flickering carbide lamps, the clatter of the miners' clogs, the gleam of quartz in the tunnel walls, and the warmth underground that, once the miners could get through the snowdrifts of Mosedale, allowed them to work in shirtsleeves. The ore was pushed to the surface in wheeled, wooden tubs, processed in the Mosedale works, and then carried by steam waggon to the railway at Troutbeck.

Ian Tyler records that in 1916 an innocent geologist was spotted on the summit of Coomb Height, overlooking the strategic tungsten mines. The villagers of Mosedale seized the man as a German spy and imprisoned him in the schoolroom overnight.

In 1919 the price of tungsten dropped again. The mine closed, to await the next world war.

This duly came. In 1942, the fall of Burma to the Japanese cut off the Allies' main supply of tungsten, now even more important in the age of tank warfare. The Carrock Fell Mine was recommissioned by a company of Canadian military sappers. The age of the waterwheel was now almost over. A diesel compressor was to power the mine machinery: although when it was first fired up, its flywheel flew out through the gable end of the building and propelled itself down Mosedale.

In 1944, with the winning of the Battle of the Atlantic against the German submarines, American tungsten was available again and the mines closed down.

Over 50 years, the enemies of Britain had been the best of friends to the Carrock mining enterprise. But in 1953, the mine found an enemy of its own, when attempts to reopen it were thwarted by the brand-new Lake District National Park Authority, along with the National Trust. Mining was ugly, dirty and dangerous. Beatrix Potter's Lakeland ought to support itself with tearooms and subsidised sheep-farming.

By 1971 the national park had relaxed its attitude to what is a traditional industry of Lakeland going back five centuries. With the price of tungsten high and stable, the Carrock Fell Mine prepared to reopen, recruiting 23 miners with ancient Lakeland surnames but shaggy 1970s hairstyles. As the first ore emerged into Mosedale the tungsten price collapsed. The mine closed again in August 1972. It reopened in 1976, and operated profitably until 1981. The world price of the metal once again collapsed, and the Carrock Mine closed for the fifth time – so far.

In Lakeland, much is preserved artificially and for our benefit: the slate houses, the Herdwick sheep, the antique road system. It's strange to think of an authentic 19th century industry, in defiance of both economics and the national park authority, sneakily establishing itself in the heart of our hills no more than 30 years ago. Wainwright arrived on Carrock Fell with pipe, camera and sketchbook in 1961 (or possibly 1960). Since his time, the mine has reopened itself, run for seven years, and then vanished, all in the middle of the fellwalking age. In 1989 its buildings were bulldozed away. Today, the holes in the hill are collapsing and filled up with rubble.

The Spiral River and the Tarn of Immortal
Talking Fish: life's a little bit different
at the Back of Blencathra.

Composite image of the 'Back of Blencathra' from Berrier Hill, in January just before sunrise

8. BACK OF BLENCATHRA
BANNERDALE, BOWSCALE FELL AND MUNGRISDALE COMMON

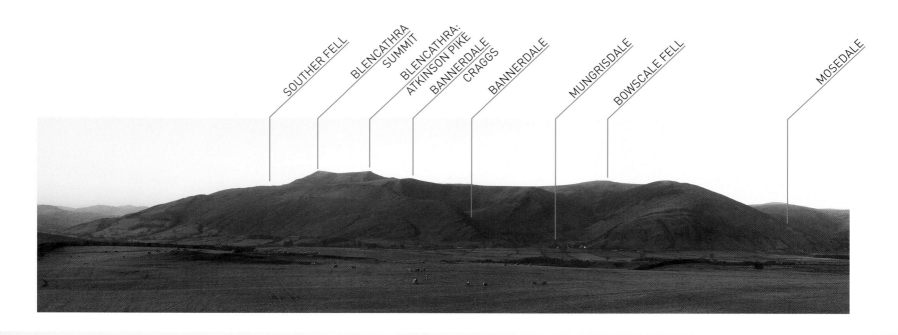

SOUTHER FELL · BLENCATHRA SUMMIT · BLENCATHRA: ATKINSON PIKE · BANNERDALE CRAGGS · BANNERDALE · MUNGRISDALE · BOWSCALE FELL · MOSEDALE

To the East and North of Saddleback there is a continuation of several hills of less note, principally covered with heath and disagreeable to the eye, which are terminated in the open cultivated part of the country. The most remarkable of these are Souter-fell, Bowscale-fell, Carrock-fell, and Caldbeck fells.

– Housman, *Description of Cumberland, Westmoreland, etc.* 1800

"Life is Like a Box of Chocolates" says Forrest Gump in a line that's been voted one of movie-goers' 10 most hated of all time. And if that's so, then Lakeland is like Life. Every One Is Different, and You Never Know What You Gonna Get. In Life, I find, there's never anything left but the one with the big Brazil nut in it. In Lakeland, however, you come back to the box again and again and still find such treats as the Bannerdale Cracker and the Bowscale Delight.

Parts of Lakeland, of course, are that box of chocolates after it's been carried in the rucksack through a long summer's day. The Back of Skiddaw is brown and slightly too squelchy. But Blencathra is better than its neighbour Skiddaw, and it also has a better Back. The Lakeland Variety Pack has at least a dozen completely different sorts of place; the land at the Back o' Blencathra is smooth but steep, with long elegant ridges, and interestingly shaped hollows between.

You don't know about it because it's hidden away by Souther Fell, but here behind Blencathra is one of Lakeland's most spacious side-valleys. Bannerdale is a wide half-mile of empty air. It's Skiddaw Slate country in the Northern Fells, so Bannerdale surrounds its empty air with swooping lines of grass and just a fringe of crag – which makes it feel even bigger than it is.

Bannerdale is formed as a complex rounded hollow, as if several helpings of hill have been removed with a super-sized ice cream scoop. It's a well-shaped space, a cosy enclosure for early morning walkers. Or it would be if those walkers hadn't already got their feet wet in Bannerdale's soggy bottom. As well as a large number of rushes and a few sheepfolds, Bannerdale has some abandoned lead mines and one abortive one for graphite, far less famous than the graphite mines of Borrowdale.

Heading for Blencathra over Bannerdale Crags is not a very popular option, but has two good reasons for it. The first is the start point in charming

Mungrisdale village, where even the parking charges are quaintly undersized. The second is the way the ascent is broken into two sections, with a scenic grassy wander as the interlude.

But Bannerdale is where alternative routes onto Blencathra stray into the absurd – as well as into those deep soggy rushes. For having sensibly decided on the Bannerdale attack, there are still at least five ways to do it.

To save standing around in the damp, the best of them is Bannerdale Crags' east ridge. Straight away it lifts you off the valley's soggy floor onto a rounded spur. At its head, you pass a minor mine building, then confront the steeper rib which divides the rocky face like the nose between two hard-living elderly eyebrows. The spur offers a little scrambling along its crest, or there's a very small path to the left. Either way, you arrive suddenly at the crag top, just a few steps from one of the summit cairns.

The alternatives are the almost-mathematically graded path on the southern flank of the Tongue; the Tongue's main face, which is rather steep; and Bowscale Fell's east ridge, which is also steep above the north end of Mungrisdale village, but then unfolds into a long, almost horizontal wander. The fifth way is by Bowscale Tarn, and an old path that slants to the right across its headwall onto its western spurline. None of these lines is bad, and for a fifteenth or twentieth ascent of Blencathra it's advisable to simply permute them all until exhausted.

For all of the Bannerdale beginnings, the continuation is across the col at the head of Glenderamackin, and then by the steep, scenic spur to Foule Crag. There's a fairly well-formed zig-zag path up what's named on large-scale maps as Blue Screes.

BOWSCALE TARN

There are only two tarns in the Northern Fells: but both of them are beauties. Scales Tarn under Blencathra spreads its waters across this book's first section. But in Victorian times, Bowscale Tarn was the popular one. Indeed, it's the finest tarn in all Lakeland, supposing you only count those that can be reached by ladies wearing long tweed skirts and riding on ponies. It's your classic corrie tarn, with a crag wall at its back, steepness all around, and a lumpy moraine barrier across the foot.

Scales Tarn is not the only place celebrated as reflecting the stars at noonday. Green's Guide quotes an even earlier writer, Mr Smith:

"Bowscale Tarn," says Mr. Smith, " is a lake near a mile in circumference, three miles north east

Blencathra summit and Atkinson Pike, from Bowscale Fell.

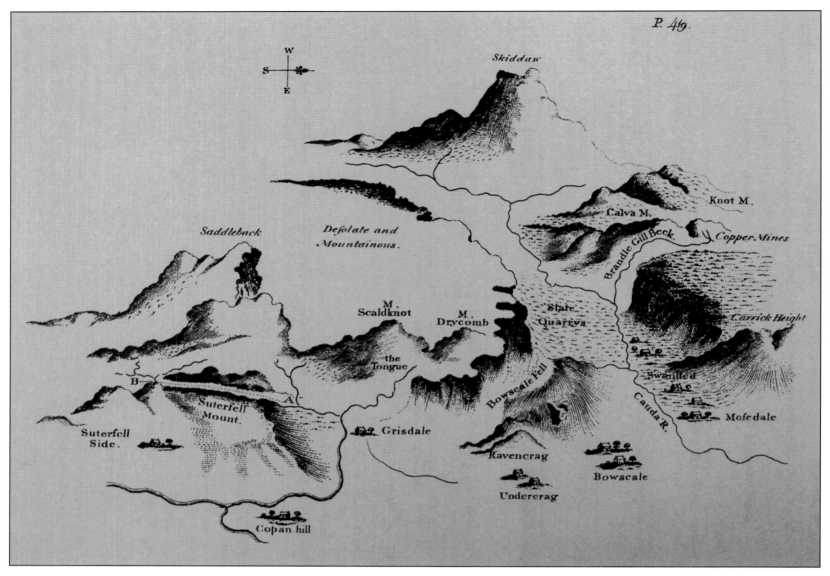

Labels on the map: P. 419. · W S E (compass) · Skiddaw · Knot M. · Calva M. · Copper Mines · Saddleback · Desolate and Mountainous. · Brandle Gill Beck · Carrick Height · M. Scaldknot · M. Drycomb · Slate Quarrys · B · the Tongue · Swaffled · A · Suterfell Mount. · Bowscale Fell · Cauda R. · Mosedale · Suterfell Side. · Grisdale · Ravencrag · Bowscale · Undercrag · Copan hill

of Scales Tarn, on the side of a high mountain, so strangely surrounded with a more eminently amphitheatrical ridge of quarry rocks, that it excluded the benefit of the sun for at least four months in the middle of winter ; but this is not its only singularity. Several of the most credible inhabitants thereabouts affirming that they frequently see stars in it at midday : but in order to discover that phenomenon the firmament must be perfectly clear, the air stable and the water unagitated. These circumstances not concurring at the time I was there, deprived me of the pleasure of that sight, and of recommending it to the naturalist upon my own ocular evidence. The spectator must be placed at least two hundred yards above the lake, and as much below the summit of the semiambient ridge ; and as there are other high mountains, which in that position may break and deaden the solar rays, I can only give an implicit credit to the power of their agency till I am convinced of their effects, and am qualified to send it better recommended to the public."

If the starry firmament is ever during daylight reflected in the still waters of the lakes, envolved in inverted cones of crags ; Mr. Otley and the writer like the above explorists, have hitherto been unfortunate in their visits to such places; and of the reality of these spectacles, they must think doubtingly till favoured by visual demonstration.

– William Green, *Guide to the Lakes*, 1818

Back o' Blencathra in 1794, from Hutchinson's History of Cumberland: *book illustration by courtesy of Carlisle Library*

And under its waters live two immortal fish. Their names are disclosed as Adam and Eve by Eliza Lynn Linton, writing in 1864. In 1864 everyone knew they were there, and what their names were, and everyone knew someone else who'd actually seen them. Wordsworth describes them vividly: "glancing, gleaming, dark or bright, moved to and fro for his delight". Poetic imagination, or an actual sighting of what could be two unusually large, and of course everlasting, trout?

View up Bannerdale from Mungrisdale. The shadow line picks out the east ridge of Bannerdale Crags, an attractive ascent route.

CLIFFORD'S CLIFFS

The one person who is on record as having seen the immortal fish, and even held conversation with them, was Henry Clifford, a nobleman turned fellwalker of the Middle Ages. His father, Lord John Clifford of Brougham, had belonged to the Lancastrian faction. When he was killed outside Wakefield Castle at the battle of Towton, his wife and child fled into the hills. The boy grew up as a shepherd on the estate of his uncle, Sir Launcelot Threlkeld.

> Now who is he that bounds with joy
> On Carrock's side, a shepherd boy?
> No thoughts hath he but thoughts that pass
> Light as the wind along the grass…
> And both th' undying fish that swim
> Through Bowscale-tarn did wait on him….
> Love had he found in huts where poor men lie;
> His daily teachers had been woods and rills,
> The silence that is in the starry sky,
> The sleep that is among the lonely hills.

Wordsworth describes him chatting not only with the two immortal fish, but also with the fairies of Carrock Fell, and studying astronomy from the useful viewpoint of Sharp Edge.

After the Lancastrian victory at Bosworth in 1485, the young Lord Henry returned to his estates. However, his time at the Back of Blencathra had permanently changed him. Instead of charging over the countryside murdering people, as was proper for those of his social standing, he stayed at home to rebuild his castles at Brougham, Brough, and Pendragon near Kirkby Stephen.

Fellwalking remained in the family. When the castles fell during the Civil War of the 1640s, they were again rebuilt by Lord Henry's last descendant. Lady Anne Clifford travelled across the moors between her various castles. Today she's remembered by her fellow-walkers for a trail linking Skipton to Penrith through the Yorkshire Dales and along the limestone edges of Cumbria. Those for whom the 100 miles (160km) of Lady Anne's Way are a bit too far could trek instead to Bowscale Tarn, to see if they can see the immortal talking fish.

MUNGRISDALE COMMON: THE WORST WAINWRIGHT

And yet, while celebrating all these interesting places at the Back of Blencathra, one awkward lump of peat and heather keeps blocking the line of our argument; just as, on the actual fellside, it blocks any path between Blencathra and its interesting back country. Mungrisdale Common is not an interesting place.

It could be questioned whether Mungrisdale Common is even a place. At 633m, it is 60m lower than any nearby hill and 235m lower than Blencathra. It does, however, manage to be six metres higher than the Caldbeck TV mast. It covers a lot of the map, but when seen from the side it only rises by 10m from the sloping northern slope of its parent hill. It has not a single closed contour line to call its own. It does have its name – and, more importantly, its chapter of six pages in A. Wainwright's *Northern Fells*.

Not all of the summits listed in Wainwright's great work are equally worthwhile. Not all of them are even summits. Bonscale Pike, perched on the ridge-edge above Ullswater, only looks like somewhere when seen from down at the lake side. Bonscale Pike does, however, have a fine view of that lake. Mungrisdale Common has a glimpse of a corner of Derwent Water, seen through the gap of Glenderaterra. That glimpse of the real Lakes country only goes to worsen the rest of the panorama; the shapeless lumps of Great Calva and High Pike, the less exciting side of Skiddaw, and the acres of grass that make the back slope of Blencathra.

Some people don't like Dodd. Dodd, the western foothill of Skiddaw, is climbed on plantation roads under gloomy spruce and larch. A muddy path, strengthened with slippery spruce roots, led up to a pitiful little cairn. Around it, on all four sides, dead twigs and pinecones concealed a view of all central Lakeland, two Lakes, the sea and Scotland. But that felltop has now been felled, destroying any claim of Dodd to be the dreariest.

Some may say that Grike, in the deserted West behind Haycock, isn't awfully exciting. Grike is a featureless grassy lump – but it does have a view of Ennerdale, as well as that wonderful name. Anyway, there are worse things than featureless grassy lumps. There are featureless heather lumps; and Little Mell Fell is even less exciting than Grike.

However, Little Mell Fell is made of a pinkish concrete washed out of the canyons of a 10,000ft range of sandstone mountains which stood on top of Lakeland in the Devonian era. Even to non-

geologists, the Mell Fell Conglomerate must be slightly fascinating.

You struggle up Armboth Fell through four hundred feet of trees. But at the forest fence everything changes. Below the fence, it was unpleasantly steep: above, it is flat. Below, it was bare rock and long grass: above, it's bracken, bog and heather. Some time after falling in the peat hole you start to wonder why you haven't arrived at any hill yet. You wipe the mud off the map and work out which of the wandering contours is up. Half a mile behind you, beyond a whole lot of deep heather, is a wide flat place on the side of High Tove. That was it: Armboth Fell. Even so, it's no use just tramping over to the little 480m contour-ring on the plateau where the Harvey's map marks the cairn.

THIS PAGE: Red waxcap (Hygrocybe) toadstool, (bottom) and autumn ground cover of reindeer moss and bilberry at about 600m on the Tongue of Bowscale Fell (top).
OPPOSITE: Across Bowscale Tarn to Carrock Fell. The moraine hump across the corrie rim means that the reverse view isn't possible: the waters of Bowscale Tarn cannot be seen from Carrock.

The Armboth plateau has seven 480m contour rings. Whichever of the seven knolls you stand on, one of the others is higher. For the full Armboth experience, plod round them all.

Armboth Fell is so nasty it's actually quite exciting. Nowhere else will you get mudstained legs right up to the level of your neck. Scafell Pike, Blencathra: for anybody reasonably fit, there's no problem with them. Under various possible weather conditions, Scafell Pike and Blencathra are actually enjoyable. Armboth Fell is something else again.

But there's nothing so unusual about Mungrisdale Common. The bogs on Mungrisdale Common are common bogs. They wet the feet but fail to threaten death. Earnest fellwalkers have brought stones from afar to form a cairn – for it is, after all, listed in Wainwright. The weight of these stones has sunk that summit cairn so that it no longer stands, if it ever did, at the domed bog's high point. Instead, it stands in a puddle.

Unwell on Ill Crag, or even worse on Barf? Wondering if Great Cockup could be a Wainwright mistake? Try the one that's the peak of imperfection: the fell that refused to get up again. It's less great than Great Sca Fell. It's less exciting than Grike. It lacks the slime and stimulating nastiness of Armboth Fell. There's no worse Wainwright than Mungrisdale Common.

ABOVE: Bannerdale from Berrier Hill.
OPPOSITE: Bannerdale, and the enjoyable east ridge of Bannerdale Crags. Present-day Threlkeld Hall, below Doddick Gill on Blencathra (left). Solufluction, the downhill creep of soil under freeze-and-thaw action, has formed these terraces at the top of Bannerdale Crags' east ridge (right).

THE SHAPE OF LAKELAND

Walkers spend our time on Lakeland hills in the middle mostly. It's only when we get on one of the edge-hills – Dent or Loadpot; Bannerdale Crags or Carrock Fell – that we notice how well-defined that edge is. Other ranges peter out into the Lowlands. But Lakeland, on its western, northern and northeast sides, stops suddenly.

As you stand on Carrock, the ground falls in scree and small crags. But 1500ft below, the last small stones of the scree roll out onto flat farmland. The national park boundary more-or-less follows this clear fell edge all the way round; dividing the sheep slope from the cow field, the walking boot from the Wellington. It also marks an alteration in the rock. The crags and screes of Carrock are mountain rock in grey, purple and black. The field edges below are walled with beige limestone.

The geological story behind the shape of Lakeland comes in three chapters.

STAGE 1 (250 million years ago)
The rocks at the bottom, coloured grey and purple, were once the roots of the Caledonian mountain chain. This is tough stuff, compressed and hardened by the earth movements that raised those long-ago mountains. But it's been there for 250 million years already and a couple of geological ages of wind and rain have worn it down as flat as East Anglia.

On top is a layer of limestone, deposited when, Lakeland, was underwater in the Carboniferous era, 350 million years ago.

On top of the limestone is a layer of sandstone, deposited when 'Lakeland' was surfaced with desert dunes in the Permian era of only 280 million years ago.

STAGE 2 (30 million years ago)
Far away in the Mediterranean, Africa is banging against the bottom of Italy, and the top of Italy is being squashed up into Europe; the crash zone is becoming the Alps. Pull one corner of the tablecloth and you get ripples everywhere else. In a similar way, the crash at the corner of Africa causes northwest England to rise into a dome.

STAGE 3 (today)
The softer limestone and sandstone have eroded right away. And so the ancient rocks of the Caledonian mountain chain get to stage a come-back. These are now the Skiddaw slates and Borrowdale Volcanics of the Lake District hills. Drive away along the A66, and the limestone makes roadside walls from Penruddock onwards. And you'll be reaching the Permian Era at Penrith with its blood-red sandstone castle.

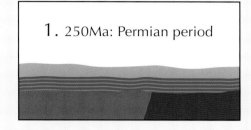

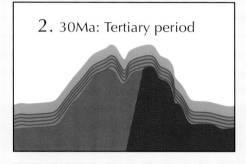

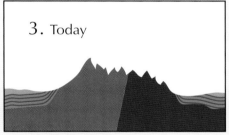

Looking over the edge of Lakeland – down the east ridge of Bowscale Fell towards Greystoke Forest and Penrith.

ABOVE: Blencathra from Knott, with Mungrisdale Common the low hump in front.

OPPOSITE: The cairn on Mungrisdale Common, and Skiddaw (top).
Cairns built by shepherds are considerably better crafted. This one, between the summit and the Cloven Stone, probably marks a break in the slope from which sheep can be overseen both above and below (bottom).

Mungrisdale Common summit on an autumn evening, looking up to Atkinson Pike.

PREVIOUS PAGES: Steep slate strata at the back of Bannerdale Crags; the slope overlooking Glenderamackin, seen from the beck below Scales Tarn (p.146). Evening sheep above Mungrisdale Common (p.147 top). From Bowscale Fell, looking out along the gap of Mosedale to the Pennines 25 miles away across the Vale of Eden (p.147 bottom).

*Atkinson Pike with Foule Crag, from the peaty col
between Bowscale Fell and Bannerdale Crags.
The left-hand ridges are Sharp Edge, below,
and Scales Fell, the skyline.*

*Bowscale Tarn, with a view
across Mosedale to High Pike*

The Glenderamackin is a tricky one to spell or to say, but that's nothing to what it's like to follow on the ground. Rising under the shadow of Sharp Edge, it runs southeast, then northeast, then north alongside Souther Fell. It then starts to unwind itself by turning south, and then west, changes its name to the Greta, and ends up in Keswick – having travelled in every direction there is, and most of them twice over.

Souther Fell from the east. The Glenderamackin emerges from behind Souther Fell to flow (right to left) across the foreground. Upstream, it curves round from behind Bannerdale Crags (clouded, at right).

9. SOUTHER FELL AND GLENDERAMACKIN
MUNGRISDALE VILLAGE

SOUTHER FELL

GLENDERAMACKIN

MUNGRISDALE VILLAGE

MACKIN' TRACKS – THE WANDER ALONG THE SPIRAL RIVER

The Glenderamackin is a tricky one to spell or to say, but that's nothing to what it's like to follow on the ground. Rising under the shadow of Sharp Edge, it runs southeast, then northeast, then north alongside Souther Fell. A further turn to the left and it'd make Bowscale Fell into an island and itself into a circular river like something in a picture by Max Escher. Accordingly it now starts to unwind itself by taking a turn to the right.

This brings a new problem. By running east it has accidentally left the Lake District. Accordingly it turns south, and then west, changes its name to the Greta, and ends up in Keswick – having travelled in every direction there is, and most of them twice over.

To make tracks up the spiral river, you start at Mungrisdale – a name that's almost as nice as Glenderamackin. A sign points to Mungrisdale Common: this would eventually be reached, but by a route so roundabout and twisting as to prevent even the greediest of villagers from overgrazing with his personal herd or flock. An old miners' path, the most comfortable of walking, gives a great view of the Bannerdale Crags and then leads into the narrow green slot. Steep sides make sure you've no idea where the next bend is going to take you. And then, high overhead, appears Sharp Edge of Blencathra. From here it looks particularly satisfying – if you've already done Sharp Edge – and particularly scary – if you haven't but have always been meaning to.

At last, the nick in the skyline that's the source of the river appears far ahead. The way up to the pass looks far too far and high even to fit into these smaller hills – but in fact the pass is closer than it looks. In this country of spiral rivers and everlasting fish, why be surprised at a path that gets smaller as it rises to deceive the eye?

In this last stretch of the valley, directly below Sharp Edge, is the Saddleback Old Mine. This was worked in the 18th century, but reopened in 1825, which was when the good access track was built up the Glenderamackin. From the track you can see the outline of the mine building just below. Between it and the stream was the dressing floor, and on the slope opposite is the evidence of 18th century hushing: release of dammed waters from above to expose bedrock. There are also traces of the leat which ran in from the Scales Tarn Beck. The mine

The head of Glenderamackin, from the foot of Sharp Edge. The old mine track continues above the mines themselves (off right edge of the picture, directly below the photographer) to the valley head.

rubble includes bright orange-yellow crystals of limonite, an iron ore.

The spiral Glenderamackin succeeded in mystifying the mine owners. The land on the Blencathra (west) side of the stream, which contained the lead vein, actually belonged to Lord Lowther – the landowner to the east – rather than to Lord Lonsdale of Greystoke, to whom they were paying rent. Rather than trying to unwind the river, the two Lords agreed to go halves.

Surprisingly, the well-built mine path continues beyond the old mine, right up to the top of the valley. Possibly some mineworkers commuted by using the high way, over the col from the Caldew. Alternatively it may communicate with the building now ruined, and itself mysterious, on the moorland slope above Mungrisdale Common (grid ref: NY318290).

The path emerges suddenly from the enclosed stream top of Glenderamackin. There's a feeling of wide spaces, as the Caldew valley opens ahead. On the right, a short, gentle slope leads to the grassy plateau of Bannerdale Crags and Bowscale Fell. To left, a scarcely steeper ridge leads to Foule Crag and the end of Blencathra. Ahead, the ground becomes the gentle grassland of the Back of Skiddaw. There is, it has to be admitted, a bit of a bog up here. You'll just have to look around and enjoy the view. Blencathra itself appears from this direction as a fine pointed peak; the great hollow of the Caldew; behind, the long slot of the Glenderamackin, and then the Vale of Eden stretches all the way across to the Pennines – oops, I'm afraid you got distracted and walked into a bit of that bog...

MUNGRISDALE

Mungrisdale village can be identified as lying half way to the Back of Beyond – or to the Back of Skiddaw, which is perhaps the same thing. This is reflected in the car parking charges. In central Lakeland: £5. In Caldbeck: no charge. In Mungrisdale, parking is £2 per car, currently payable into a home-made honesty box rather than an unsightly pay-and-display machine.

The Mill Inn is 17th-century, and many of the village houses are former farms of about the same age. The sawmill and smithy were briefly busy during the working life of the Carrock Fell Mine; the Mill Inn even more so. Despite its part in the war effort, the sawmill continued to be powered by a waterwheel through the 1940s. Its site is now the inn car park.

Mungrisdale's church has a remarkable amount of lichen and moss for so small a building. Inside it has a triple-decker pulpit that would allow three vicars to preach simultaneously, one above the

ABOVE: Looking across Glenderamackin from the Scales Tarn beck. The old track runs across the base of Bannerdale Crags: the Old Blencathra Mine is below the track, at centre (left).
The mine track continues down valley around the base of Bannerdale Crags (right).
BELOW: Saddleback Old Mine, with Sharp Edge above. At the foot of the slope opposite the mine building, the lines of two former leats run across at different levels, each of them rising very gradually to the left (top). Limonite, an iron ore, at Old Blencathra Mine (bottom).

other. It is dedicated to St Mungo. Mungo was a prince of Rheged whose real name was Kentigern. Mungo is a nickname, Gaelic for 'dear little puppy', that he acquired in childhood from an older saint, St Serf. Mungo was apostle to the Celtic kingdom of Strathclyde, some time in the 6th century, and is the patron saint of Glasgow. After the battle of Dunmail Raise, which (if a real event at all) happened around 945AD, northern Cumbria was incorporated into Strathclyde; and several churches survive in the area dedicated to Mungo. Local tradition, however, says that Mungo himself founded the churches while in temporary exile from Glasgow under an unchristian king.

The present building is from about 1756. Its bell is dated 1481, and Coleridge recorded in 1800 an anecdote about it. Two lads lifted the bell down with ladders and buried it. They then spread rumours as to its whereabouts, for the fun of watching the villagers haring around over the countryside looking for it. Coleridge names the pranksters in his Notebooks as Isaac Ritson and John Slee.

Mungrisdale means 'Mungo's valley of pigs', with 'Grisdal', pig valley, also the name of three other, widely-scattered, places in the Lakes – one tarn, one pike, and one forest.

SPECTRAL CINEMA

If Blencathra is a seat, then who sits in it? According to Heaton Cooper (in *The Tarns of Lakeland)* it's the same scaly-bottomed personage who sits on some shattered quartzite down in Shropshire. In which case, does Satan have a liking for slide-shows?

At the Devil's Chair on Shropshire's Stiperstones, Wild Eldric and his ghostly horde have been seen flitting across the hillside. At Souther Fell below Blencathra, on Midsummer Eve in 1735, in 1737 and in 1745, horsemen and carriages moved rapidly

across the face of the hill and then disappeared.

Wild Eldric rides when the kingdom is in danger. 1745 was the year of Prince Charlie's invasion, when he took possession of Carlisle. So perhaps that was spectral Eldric himself flitting across the face of Souther Fell? Or perhaps it was just cloud shadows under the moon; or even the Brocken Spectre.

I described the Brocken Spectre in Section 3 – Blencathra is the only place where I've seen the spectre twice over. But I've never seen Prince Charlie's army. So I'll go back to the first written account I can find; which happens to be a very early work of Wordsworth.

> Strange apparitions mocked the shepherd's sight.
> The form appears of one that spurs his steed
> Midway along the hill with desperate speed;
> Unhurt pursues his lengthened flight, while all
> Attend, at every stretch, his headlong fall.
> Anon, appears a brave, a gorgeous show
> Of horsemen-shadows moving to and fro;
> At intervals imperial banners stream,
> And now the van reflects the solar beam;
> The rear through iron brown betrays a sullen gleam.
> While silent stands the admiring crowd below,

> Silent the visionary warriors go,
> Winding in ordered pomp their upward way
> Till the last banner of the long array
> Has disappeared, and every trace is fled
> Of splendour—save the beacon's spiry head
> Tipt with eve's latest gleam of burning red.

An Evening Walk, dedicated to his sister Dorothy, was written during 1787-89, his last year at school and his two years at Cambridge. 'Attend' carries its old meaning, of await or expect: 'Van' is vanguard, the front end of the army. The long poem describes the sights and sounds and, especially, the changing light of a Lakeland day. In notes written 50 years later he claims: "There is not an image in it which I have not observed". But this presumably was not meant to apply to the phantom horsemen, who are described in the same notes as a "Superstition of the Country connected with that moment [sunset]".

The 'beacon' is presumably Skiddaw: for the hill of the phantoms, though not named by Wordsworth, is Souther Fell. The details of the 'Superstition of the Country' are the same as in the account five years later in Hutchinson's *History of Cumberland*; from which, presumably, all later ones have been transcribed and embellished.

On Midsummer Eve, 1735, a servant in the employ of William Lancaster, of Blakehills, about half a mile from Souterfell, related that he saw the east side of

The view that makes Saddleback into a quite different sort of mountain. Atkinson Pike, the north-eastern end of the summit plateau, seen from Glenderamackin. Sharp Edge forms the left-hand skyline.

Souther Fell from the south, linked with the main mass of Blencathra by the col at the top of Mousthwaite Comb. Scales settlement and Inn are at bottom left.

the mountain, towards the summit, covered with a regular marching army for about an hour together. They consisted of distinct bodies of troops, which appeared to proceed from an eminence in the north end, and marched over a niche in the top; but as no other person in the neighbourhood had seen a similar appearance, he was discredited and laughed at.

Two years after, on midsummer eve also, William Lancaster himself imagined that several gentlemen were following their horses at a distance, as if they had been hunting; and taking them for such, paid no regard to it, till about ten minutes after, again turning his head towards the place, they appeared to be mounted, and a vast army following, five in rank, crowding over at the same place, where the servant said he saw them two years before. He then called his family, who all agreed in the same opinion ; and what was most extraordinary, he frequently observed that some one of the five would quit the ranks, and seem to stand in a fronting posture, as if he was observing and regulating the order of their march, or taking account of the numbers, and after some time appeared to return full-gallop to the station he had left, which they never failed to do as often as they quitted their lines, and the figure that did so was generally one of the middlemost men in the rank.

As it grew later, they seemed more regardless of discipline, and rather had the appearance of people riding from a market, than an army, though they continued crowding on, and marching off, as long as there was light to see them.

'Blakehills' is Blake Hills Farm on today's map, immediately below Souther Fell on the side road to Mungrisdale. The marching army reappeared on Midsummer's Eve 1745 – a significant date, as Bonnie Prince Charlie's army would capture Carlisle five months later. The Lancaster household, having been laughed at enough on the previous occasion, gathered 26 neighbours, who later affirmed before a magistrate that they had indeed seen the army: this time not just horsemen, but carriages as well. The figures on the fell did not at all resemble wafts of mist. They were not, however, real people: the ground was too steep and rocky for marching, let alone carriages; and an inspection the following morning found no hoofprints.

The long ridge of Souther Fell drops off steeply to Mungrisdale village. Its foot is defended by luxuriant and tangly bracken, and by small fields with barbed wire and unstable stone walls. So the path onto the fell actually starts 500m south of the village on the gated hill road to Scales. Once on the fell, it's an

enjoyable, almost level, ramble of 2km. The saddle of Blencathra rises far ahead and above, and wide views are south to the central fells and backwards towards the Pennines – though that one is liable to be spoilt soon by a windfarm planned for the moorland of Berrier.

Even so, Souther Fell makes an unfrequented, undemanding, and beautiful beginning to a day: one that might well continue, after the Mousthwaite col, by a scramble up Sharp Edge. Chris Bonington, climber of Everest, Annapurna, and the Old Man of Hoy, lives in this corner of Cumbria and lists Blencathra as one of his top hills in the whole world. And his favourite way up it, as described in *Classic Walks* (1982), is by Souther Fell.

ABOVE: The Scafells and Great Gable from Souther Fell, during a February sunset.
BELOW: Glenderamackin valley, just before sunrise.

TOP: The church of St Kentigern (or Mungo)
dates from about 1750 but is on a site
sanctified by St Mungo himself.
BELOW: Mill Inn, centre point of the village for
three centuries (left), Inside the church (right).

MUNGRISDALE

ABOVE: The village from the east. On the left, the steep end of Souther Fell. Behind, Bannerdale, with the east ridge running up towards Bannerdale Crags. River Glenderamackin runs out from behind Souther Fell. BELOW: Mungrisdale village seen down Bannerdale from the Tongue of Bowscale Fell

From Halls Fell top, the ridge southeast to Blease Fell is one of the best miles in England. Indeed, of miles that can be walked with so little effort, it has to be the best of all. All the way along this ridgeline, the place feels a lot more alpine than it actually is…

Blencathra seen along Borrowdale from Green Gable, 13 miles away

10. BLENCATHRA

THE SUMMIT RIDGE

The smiling vegetation at its foot, and the animated features of the middle and distant high lands as observed on the walk from Knott Crag, by Lile Fell, Priest Man, and Linthwaite Pike to Atkinson's Man, present a succession of the most amusing assemblages in the country.

William Green Guide to the Lakes 1818: the five tops are now named as Blease Fell, Gategill Fell Top, Hall's Fell Top (Blencathra summit), and Atkinson Pike.

BLENCATHRA SUMMIT

Blencathra's main summit is Halls Fell Top: at the northern end is Atkinson Pike, the high point above Sharp Edge. Between the two is a wide, flat col: the saddle that gives the defining name to Saddleback. It's the one place on the summit plateau where, on a normal sunny day, you could find yourself all alone.

The scramblers coming off Sharp Edge follow the brink of the Scales Tarn combe on a path where they can enjoy the "dreadful abyss, the bottom of which the eye could not penetrate," so appreciated by Thomas Clement and his client in 1793. Those walkers are only 100 metres away, but the curve of the hilltop takes the tops of their bobble-hats just down below the skyline and out of sight. And that same hill curve separates the col occupant from the rest of the busy Lakeland fells. Just the dim line of the Pennines, 30 miles away, rises a few inches above the stalks of grass. Look out the other way, westwards, and there's the slow curve of Skiddaw, above the meandering contours of Knott and Great Calva.

This saddle of Saddleback is a memory of a simpler, quieter and older place. It is Lakeland before there were any lakes or craggy bits. And this is not merely metaphorical. The saddle, and the rest of the Blencathra plateau, is actually a land surface from before the glaciers.

Earthquakes, volcanoes, even rain and frost, are all mere landscape tinkering. A hundred million tons of ice, embedded with boulders like the teeth of a rasp, moving unstoppably downhill over tens of thousands of years: this is Nature's really effective demolition agent. Glaciers make the big, exciting shapes of Lakeland: the crag-rimmed tarns, the steep-sided dales, the scooped hollow at the dale foot that now contains Bassenthwaite Lake or Ullswater. It's a neat paradox that it's exactly this force of total destruction that has created England's loveliest landscape.

Before the glaciers got at it, through long slow ages rain and frost had been wearing down the mountain remnant that we now call Lakeland. Rain and frost made a gently rolling, and for fellwalkers fairly boring, moorland – a moorland that sloped up the northern side of Blencathra and across its saddle. Give or take some frost-shattering of the bedrock, the downhill soil creep called solufluction, and a bit of peat, that pre-glacial moorland is still the slope we eat our sandwiches on today. 100,000 years ago, a mountain hare might have trotted up from Mungrisdale Common, crossed Hallsfell Top, and simply carried on, through the sky 600m above Threlkeld – eventually rejoining the modern landmass at the trig point on Clough Head.

Let's be optimistic and suppose that human-induced global warming will turn out, in a million years time, to have been just a blip in Earth's geological history (rather than the end of the Tertiary period, the seventh of the planet's great mass extinctions, a narrow band of fossil tea-strainers and railway engines, and the beginning of a totally different climate with limestone and ocean shells over a lot of what has previously been land). Let's hope that Earth's climate will in a few centuries or millennia return to where it was going anyway. That will mean a return of the Ice Age, briefly interrupted a mere 10,000 years ago. Snow will blow across Blencathra's saddle on the southwesterly blizzards, to drift down in the shady hollow of Scales Tarn and the corrie of Foule Crag. It will pile up there; harden; crack; and eventually flow – the glaciers are back. The two corrie glaciers resume their briefly interrupted carving of the corrie headwalls. Meanwhile the big Caldew Glacier grinds into Mungrisdale Common, and the smaller but steeper Roughton Glacier is cutting the base of Blencathra's northern slope.

The next interglacial comes, the ice melts away: but Blencathra's sometime summit plateau, gnawed from both west and east, is no more. Instead Blencathra stands slightly lower than we knew it, as a fine sharp ridgeline just north of the present crest. Will there be fellwalkers to appreciate that ridge? Or will self-awareness turn out to have been an evolutionary wrong turning like the tusks on the sabre-tooth tiger?

The glaciers return; and next time we look, there's not much Lakeland left at all.

But for the few brief millennia before the ice comes back, the ancient land surface forms its saddle from Atkinson Pike towards Blencathra summit. A sequence of small, tastefully arranged landmarks decorate the saddle. Just 100 metres from Atkinson Pike there's a second cairn, one which lines up nicely with the various tops along Blencathra's ridgeline. In

THIS PAGE: Summit ridge,
to Skiddaw (top). Ridge
westwards towards Gategill Top
(middle). Runner at the top of
Scales Fell, approaching summit
from east (bottom).
OPPOSITE: East of the summit,
with Solway Firth and Scotland
(top).Gategill Top eastwards to
the summit (middle left), Ridge
to Gategill Top, from summit
(middle right), Blencathra
summit view to Scafell Pike,
Great Gable (triangular with
snow patch), Kirk Fell, Pillar
(rocky face, snow patches),
Dale Head (scooped on right,
below horizon), Steeple, and
the Grasmoor group (to right
of Gategill Top, the foreground
summit of Blencathra). In
front, Derwent Water and
Keswick. In April, the Vale of
Keswick is spring green, but
the hills still hold their winter
browns(botttom).

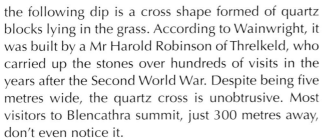

the following dip is a cross shape formed of quartz blocks lying in the grass. According to Wainwright, it was built by a Mr Harold Robinson of Threlkeld, who carried up the stones over hundreds of visits in the years after the Second World War. Despite being five metres wide, the quartz cross is unobtrusive. Most visitors to Blencathra summit, just 300 metres away, don't even notice it.

There's another cairn; then a dip is the low point of the saddle, and holds a tiny peat pool. Water seeps into it from slightly higher ground on either side, and seeps out again at either end. Only a few centimetres deep, darkened with peat and sheep droppings, in a good light it still catches the sky colour as effectively as more celebrated tarns and lakes.

A final two minutes of gentle uphill lead to a place altogether different: the trampled bare stone of Halls Fell Top, with its sudden view to the whole of the central fells. The Dodds ridgeline runs away southwards: from the hunched lump of Clough Head it becomes airier and more elegant as it rises to the tip-tilted point of Low Man and Helvellyn itself. There's a glimpse of Thirlmere; and then the jumbled mass of high fells from Coniston Old Man, by Bow Fell, to the Scafells and Great Gable. Derwent Water is seen side-on, but at an angle that still shows off some of its islands; the western fells rise behind. From nowhere in Lakeland can you see a greater spread of summits without the inconvenience of having to turn your head.

The sea can be seen to the south, west, and northwest. The long sightline is to the Mountains of Mourne, rising from the sea 120 miles away just north of the Isle of Man. Almost as distant, the Clwydian hills of Wales can occasionally be spotted, again beyond open sea, to right of Helvellyn and immediately upwards from Thirlmere.

Even so, the most impressive view is straight down. The eye drops along the shattered crest of Halls Fell to Gategill Farm, open fields, and the western half of Threlkeld.

From Halls Fell top, the ridge southeast to Blease Fell is one of the best miles in England. Indeed, of miles that can be walked on smooth wide path without steepness or rocky bits or any other sort of awkwardness, it has to be the best of all. Strictly it can be called a ridge only on its left-hand side, the side that drops in scree and slaty crag for 600 metres to the Greta and the Vale of Keswick. The northern side is no more than a grassy slope. But it's a slope that straight away curves down out of sight, giving an impression (which is in fact a false one) of empty depths leading out to the wide brown hollow of Skiddaw Forest. The cowpat contours of Great Calva and Knott are almost 200 metres lower down; the eye leaps over them to the green coastal plains and the wide waters of the Solway.

The southern side is scalloped by the deep holes of Gate Gill and Blease Gill. From any point between Hallsfell Top and Gategill Top, you can look across that first hollow to the arc of ridge you've just walked or are just about to walk; and the effect is repeated across the second hollow, between Gategill Top and Blease Fell. All the way along this ridgeline, the place feels a lot more alpine than it actually is.

And it felt even more so in the 18th century.

LEFT AND FAR RIGHT BELOW: The pool at the low point of the 'Saddleback' saddle.
ABOVE: The quartz cross east of Blencathra summit.
RIGHT, ABOVE: The cairn on Atkinson Pike.

"Here [I] came to the brink of the first of those hideous chasms which follow the southern face of this mountain … This first chasm, though by far the least formidable, is inconceivably horrid; its width is about two hundred yards, and its depth at least six hundred: after a steep and painful ascent of about a mile, I came to the brink of the other gulphs. Here a point of the mountain juts out like the angle of a bastion, between two of these horrid abysses. I stood upon this, and had on each side a gulph about two hundred yards wide, and at least eight hundred deep; their sides were rocky, bare, and rough, scarcely the appearance of vegetation upon them; and their bottoms were covered with pointed broken rocks. Passing this, I arrived at the farthest point, where the mountain has every appearance of being split; and at the bottom I saw hills about forty yards high, and a mile in length, which seem to have been raised from the rubbish that has fallen from the mountain. From hence I went to the summit, where I could see the tarn, which, as I was elevated upwards of two hundred yards above it, appeared very small: here likewise I had a most beautiful view of the country for many miles round, and could not help observing, that the back of this mountain is as remarkably smooth, as its front is horrid."
– James Clarke's *Survey of the Lakes* (1787), quoted in Hutchinson's *History of Cumberland*

The surprising thing about this account, however, is not its archaic strangeness. Coming as it does from an age when men had only just stopped off wearing wigs and silken knee-breeches, when smart people might keep a little Negro lad as a household pet, and when at the other end of society the poor even of England might die of hunger in huge numbers after a bad harvest: the strange thing about this story is how familiar it is. The four gulfs of Scales Beck, Doddick Gill, Gate Gill and Blease Gill are as exciting to gaze down into as they were 220 years ago. The remark about the gouged front and smooth back of Blencathra is repeated in Wainwright, and in most other guidebooks of today.

In the 1780s they could not entertain themselves

*Vale of Eden, Penrith and
Cross Fell, from Scales Fell*

with CDs or computer games. Music they heard only in church; the nearest they had to television was the Sunday sermon. They played cribbage and piquet, and gambled on cock fights. They watched boxing, and played whist; when they were in London, they went to see a play by Congreve or Sheridan. But one form of fun they have passed down to us through two centuries. We all like to walk up Scales Fell, and peer over the southern edge of Blencathra.

FELLRUNNER CONFRONTS BLENCATHRA: BLENCATHRA HAS THE BETTER OF IT

Mr Smith, Mr Otley, and ourselves: we all set off up Saddleback. But after 200 years of it, we don't need to make quite so much of a fuss. As a corrective to the romantic 18th-century descriptions of our hill, I close with a tale of today. The walker called 'Scasey' is considering the Bob Graham Round, the 24-hour crossing of 42 Lakeland summits. His friend Rick suggests they should preview some of the route.

Being academics we just took the next few days off and headed up to the Lakes … We got onto the top of Skiddaw with a fair bit of light remaining as I recall and then headed on a bearing-ish across that miserable ground between Skiddaw and Blencathra and I was wondering how I was ever going to get anywhere near the suggested Bob Graham times across it when we went for it for real.

On top of Blencathra it was pretty much full white out conditions and we were planning on heading down by Scales Tarn into the valley and sticking the tent up. In the "white out" we failed to pick up the tourist track, but as "luck" would have it we did manage to start heading down Sharp Edge believing it to be the tourist track. Fairly near the top the laws of physics and Rick's well worn boots conspired to take him for an enforced glissade (some 50 feet or so I would guess, but then that's like asking an angler how big his fish was). As I watched him scurry out of sight on his arse I was thinking that things were getting a little bit tasty and we opted to camp on the top of Blencathra for the night and hope things were better in the morning.

The campsite the next morning goes with one of the two quotes that will always remain with me from that trip, namely: "If anything Scasey, the weather's slightly WORSE this morning." Unfortunately the humour in that line comes mainly from the delivery which I can't really capture. The other quote, if you're

interested, was to do with a threesome Rick had managed with two random girls he picked up in a kebab house in London a week before, but isn't strictly relevant.

Nothing really happened I'm afraid, we went back to Keswick and had a couple of beers and Rick told me I was an idiot and we should never have come to the Lakes that weekend etc. etc.

Blencathra or Saddleback: in the 18th century or in a snowstorm: this summit ridge has just one shortcoming – it comes too short! Just 2km from Blease Fell to Atkinson Pike, the end of the ridgeline always arrives too early. But there are 13 more ways to return by. There are the excellent outliers of Bannerdale Crags, Bowscale and Souther Fell (not to mention Mungrisdale Common). So it's always easy to come back to Blencathra.

A 200-page book about a single hill is, of course, impossible – unless it's actually a book about people. Blencathra turns out to be one of those clubs you

ABOVE: The quartz cross lying in the saddle between Atkinson Pike and Halls Fell Top. According to A. Wainwright, it was constructed by a Mr Robinson, who made many ascents of Blencathra in the years after World War II. Quartz lumps of this size are common around the old mines at the hill foot on the Threlkeld side, and can also be found at the base of Foule Crag, on the ascent from the north. I have found none on the plateau itself. However, it may be that there were some, all of them now incorporated into this cross of stones.

wouldn't ever think of being in: the local choral society, the Rotary, the Young Women's Guild. In Blencathra's case it's a group of uncool old gents from the 19th century. In a moment of inattention you find yourself joined up (I belong to the Dalgarno Singers myself), and there's a bit of a surprise. These guys actually know a thing or two, these guys are fun!

So we have Jonathan Otley, the Keswick clockmaker, having a go at the unclimbable Sharp Edge; and in between times exploring the Caldew granite and the slates. Without the benefit of any boring geology book, Otley uncovers the chiasatolite crystals and the black spotting, and works out for the first time whether the granite crystallised out of Noah's ocean or instead arrived red-hot from underneath.

John Stuart Mill arrives on Scales Fell, his eyeballs fizzing with the visuals of this new world of mountains and cloud. Charles Dickens and Wilkie Collins knock about on Carrock in the rain, getting lost and twisting their ankles. Robert Southey, known to posterity principally as a dreadful old bore, looks at Castlerigg stone circle and actually sees it, and questions whether the early 19th century is really as clever and comfortable as it likes to make out. Even William Wordsworth, as an oddball adolescent, knows space below his hobnails, slimy handholds in

a world shrunk to a few grey inches of rock.

But above all, here is Samuel Taylor Coleridge, troubled in his stomach and already addicted to opium, but ranging across the fells like a fox. Never mind that his best poems are already all written, never mind that even his dearest friends are getting fed up. Coleridge peers at the raindrops on the moss, or looks up at a sky filled with sun shafts; and fills notebook after notebook with intense, passionate fell walking.

Coleridge had the same mind and eyeballs as we do. What he saw is there for us to see. Dawn crawls golden across the front of Blencathra, shaping the ridgelines one by one. Derwent Water burns like a bush fire in the hollow of the hills. Windblown snow makes its pattern alongside the path. Atkinson Pike hunches against the night sky; the night wind rattles the frozen grass. To know the whole world, it is enough to simply see, and be on, Blencathra.

OPPOSITE ABOVE, AND BELOW: The summit cairn gets rebuilt in a slightly different place every few years. These pictures were both taken in November of 2008.

INDEX

Page entries in *italic* represent illustrations or their captions.

Abraham, George & Ashley 9, 131
Africa, arrival of 13, 143
Alps 10, 13, 143
altitude sickness 29, 31
Annapurna 159
Armboth Fell 138–140
Atkinson Pike (Atkinson's Man) 12, *91, 127, 134, 149, 150, 157,* 165, *166–167,* 172, 173
Auden, WH 47, 55–56
Austen, Jane 29
Back o' Skiddaw 12, *20,* 27, 93, *113–114,* 120, 123–124, 135, 155 see also Carrock Fell, Great Cockup, High Pike, Knott, Roughton Gill
Back of Blencathra 9, 47, *91, 132–133,* 135–151 see also Bannerdale Crags, Bowscale Fell, Mungrisdale Common
Bakestall *100, 101, 108, 142*
Bannerdale *133,* 135, *137, 140, 141, 161*
Bannerdale Crags 6, 9, *13, 34, 43, 77, 129,* 135, *141, 143, 146–147, 153,* 155, *156,* 172
    East Ridge 135, *137, 141, 161*
beer, hill-named 123
Berrier Moor *25, 132–133, 141,* 159
Blakehills farm 157–158
Blease Fell *6,* 9, *19,* 36, *47,* 63, *66–67,* 85, *88, 91, 95,* 96, 100, 162, 165, 168, 172
Blencathra Field Centre *46,* 47, 67, *93, 95,* 100, 102
Bob Graham Round 172
Bonington, Sir Christian 110, 159
Bonscale Pike 138
Borrowdale Volcanic Series 13, 34, 125, 143
Borrowdale, Maid of 100
Bowscale Fell 6, 9, 109, *121, 126–127, 133,* 135, 138, *143, 147,* 155, *161*
Bowscale Tarn 12, *126–127,* 135–138, *139, 142,* 151
Bradbury, Julia 35–36
Brae Fell *107,* 109, *113*
Braeriach 35
Brandy Gill 125, *130,* 131
Brecon Beacons 12
Bright (Tewet) Tarn *45,* 47, 56
Bright Pavilions, The (Walpole) 47
Brocken Spectre 74, 157
Burke, Edmund 29
Burnswark Hill 10
Cadair Idris 12
Caldbeck (village) 51, 111–114, *118–119,* 131, 155
Caldbeck Fells *106–107,* 109–111, *112–113,* 115, *116–117,* 131, 135 see also Back o' Skiddaw
Caldbeck radio mast *117,* 138
Caldew, River 34, 93, 100, 114, *122,* 123, *126–127,* 155, 165, 173
campylite 110, *111*
Carrock Beck 109
Carrock Fell *6,* 9, 16, *20, 107,* 109, *116,* 120–121, 123–125, *126–129,* 135, 137, *139,* 173
    Coleridge ascends 114, 123–124
    Dickens ascends 123, 124
    geology 124–125, *129,* 143
Carrock Old Mine *130, 131,* 155

Castlerigg Stone Circle 13, *45,* 49–54, 125, 173
Catbells *22,* 93
Charlie, Bonnie Prince 157–158
chasms, inconceivably horrid 169
chiastolite *100,* 101, *102*
Clarke, James 169
Classic Walks (Wilson et al 1982) 159
Clifford, Lady Anne 136
Clifford, Lord Henry 47, 137–138
Clough Head *45, 50,* 56, 65, 67, 93, *121,* 165, 168
Clwydian Hills 168
Coleridge (Samuel Taylor) 31, 34, 47, 51, 54, 156, 173
    at Scales Tarn 31
    at the Howk 114
    on Carrock Fell 123–124
    on the Brocken 74
    quoted 18, 47, 49, 55, 114, 123
Collins, Wilkie 123–124, 173
Colloquies (Southey) 51
Columbus, Christopher 109
Concise Description of the English Lakes (Otley, 1818) 34
Coniston 100
Coniston Fault *92,* 93, *94*
Coniston Old Man 35, 168
cordierite 101–102
Cumbria Way 93, 125
Cummerland Talk (Richardson) 56
Dale Beck (Caldbeck) *107, 116–117, 118*
Dale Head *167*
Dartmoor 12, 102
Derwent Water 9, 17, *22–23,* 35, *45,* 51, *57, 60–61,* 67, *78,* 93, *104–105,* 138, *167,* 168, 173
Devil (the Christian) 47, 156
Devil's Chair, Shropshire 156
Dickens, Charles 123–124, 173
diorite 125, *129*
Dodd (Skiddaw) 138
Doddick Fell 16, *38–39, 45,* 63, 66, 67, 69, *70, 71*
Doddick Gill 74, *77, 79–81,* 88, *141,* 169
Driggeth Mine 109
Drygill *13,* 110, *111*
Dunmail Raise, Battle of 156
erosion surface 165
Escher, Max 155
Evening Walk, An (Wordsworth) 157
Everest 36, 159
Eycott Volcanics *129*
fell running 66, *166,* 172
fish, immortal talking 136–138, 155
Foule Crag 28, 36, 135, *150,* 155, *172*
Frances, St, of Assisi 36
Friedrich, Caspar David *64*
gabbro 124–125, *129*
Gate Gill 74, *77,* 80–84, *85, 89,* 168, 169
Gategill Farm 80, 83, 85, 86, 168
Gategill Fell 16, *63,* 66, 68, *72*
Gategill mines 47, 80, 82–84
Gategill Top 9, *18, 25,* 165, *166, 167,* 168, *174*
Gilpin, William 10
glaciers 13, 27, 47, 65, 93, 100, 165
Glenderamackin 27, *28, 44–45, 71,* 93, *146, 153, 154,* 155, *156, 159, 161*
Glenderaterra 16, *90–93, 94–95, 99,* 100–101, *103,* 138

Glory (optical effect) 74
geology
    Borrowdale Volcanic Series 13, 34, 125, 143
    Blencathra erosion surface 165
    Carrock Fell 124–125, *129,* 143
    Coniston Fault *92,* 93, *94*
    Eycott Volcanics *129*
    gabbro 124–125, *129*
    glaciers 13, 27, 47, 65, 93, 100, 165
    hornfels 100, 102
    limestone 13, 100, 114, 137, 143
    Mell Fell Conglomerate 138
    metamorphic areole 100
    Skiddaw Granite 12, *13,* 34, 96–102, 173
    Skiddaw Slates (Skiddaw System) 9, 13–16, 34, 96, 100–102, 135, *143,* 172–173
    Threlkeld Microgranite *45, 88, 89*
    vein breccia *85*
granite
    Carrock Fell 9, 125, *129*
    Castlerigg stones mistaken for 49
    Skiddaw 12, *13,* 34, 96–102, 173
    Threlkeld Microgranite *45, 88, 89*
Grasmoor *8, 14–15,* 16, *19, 167*
gravity, force of 100
Great Calva *20,* 94, *97, 108, 112,* 138, 165, 168
Great Cockup 123, 140
Great Gable 16, 17, 65, 123, *159, 167,* 168
Great Mell Fell *7,* 27, *29, 38, 45, 50*
Green, William 12, 34–35, 47, 135–136, 165
Greenah Crag Farm *25*
Greta, River *46,* 47, 54–55, 155, 168
Griffin, A Harry 115
Grike (Ennerdale) 138
Grisedales 156
Guide to the Lakes (West, 1778) 51, 54
Guide to the Lakes (Green, 1818) 12, 34–35, 47, 135–136, 165
Gump, Forrest 135
hairstyles, 1970s 131
hairstyles, on TV 36
Halls Fell *6,* 9, 12, 16, *25,* 63, 65–66, *68,* 73, 74, *75,* 76, *77,* 79, 80, 168
Halls Fell Top (Blencathra summit) *6,* 12, 162, 165, 168
Harding Vein (Carrock) *130*
Haystacks 36
Heaton Cooper, W 156
Helvellyn 13, 16–17, 49, 66, 93, 168
Hesket Newmarket 111, 123, 125
High Pike *6, 13, 20, 107,* 109, *121,* 123, 138, *151*
    gossip 110
    mines 109–111
    routes described 125
High Rigg, Blencathra from *4–5, 17,* 56, *63, 87*
Hindscarth 124
History of Cumberland (Hutchinson, 1794) 27–28, 48, 109, *114,* 136, 157, 169
hornfels 100, 102
Horse and Farrier (Threlkeld) 47, *59,* 66
Howk, the (Caldbeck) 114–115
humanity, possible extinction 165
Hyperion (Keats) 51–54
Iapetus Ocean 13
Ice Age 13, 93, 165 see also Glaciers

Idle Tour of Two Lazy Apprentices (Dickens) 123–124
Isle of Man 168
Jesty, Chris 36
Keats, John 51–54
Kentigern, St see Mungo
Kirk Fell *167*
Knott (Caldbeck Fells) *107, 112, 113, 114,* 165, 168
Knott Halloo 66, *72,* 86, *87*
Lake District National Park Authority 110, 131
Lake District National Park boundary 111, 143
Lancaster, William, spectre-spotter 157–158
limestone 13, 100, 114, 137, 143
limonite 155, *156*
Linthwaite Pike 12, 165
Linton, Eliza Lynn 136
Little Mell Fell 138
Lone Ranger, the 86
Lonscale Fell *6,* 93, *95, 101*
Lonsdale, Lord 155
Lowther, Lord 155
Lowthwaite Fell *107*
Macaulay, Thomas 51
Maid of Buttermere 100, 114
Malverns 47
mass extinctions 165
Maxwell, James Clerk 74
Meal Fell 109
Mell Fell Conglomerate 138
Mesopotamia 12
metamorphic areole 100
mica 16, 100
microgranite, Threlkeld *89*
Middle Tongue 84
Mill Inn, Mungrisdale 155, *160*
Mill, John Stuart 17, 31–34, 173
minerals *13,* 16, 100–102, 109–111
    campylite 110, *111*
    chiastolite *100,* 101, *102*
    cordierite 101–102
    limonite 155, *156*
    mica 16, 100
    pyromorphite 111
    tungsten (wolfram) 17, 125, 131
Mines of Lakeland Exploration Society 110
Mosedale 93, *112,* 113, 125, *128–129, 130,* 131, *133, 147, 151*
Mosedale village 131
Mountains (Auden) 55
Mourne, Mountains of 168
Mousthwaite Comb and col 9, *28, 29,* 66, *158,* 159
    route described 27
Mungo, St *118–119,* 155–156, *160*
Mungrisdale Common *6,* 12, *103–104,* 113, 138–140, *142, 144, 145, 147, 148–149,* 155, 165, 172
Mungrisdale village *6, 13,* 100, *133,* 135, 137, *153,* 155–156, 158, *161–162*
National Trust 131
Natural England 93
Naughley, Rev Alexander 48
Oddfellow's Arms, Caldbeck 115, *118*
Old Coach Road *50,* 56
Old Crown Round 123
Old Crown, Hesket Newmarket 123
Otley, Jonathan 34–35, 136, 172–173
parsley fern *129*
Pattinson's Level *111*

Peel, John, huntsman 109, 114–116, *118–119*
Pennines 9, *50,* 128, *147,* 155, 159, 165
Penrith 10, *13, 50,* 55, 137, 143, *170*
Philosophical Enquiry (Burke) 29
picturesque beauty 10
Pillar 9, 125, *167*
Potter, Beatrix 51, 131
Powder House (Gategill mines) *83,* 84
Powell-Thompson, David 36
pranksters 49, 156
Prelude, The (Wordsworth) 34
pyromorphite 111
quartz cross 168, *169, 172*
Radcliffe, Ann 47
railway, Keswick 54–55
Richardson, John 55–56
Ritson, Isaac, prankster 156
Robinson, Harold, quartz-carrier 168
Robson, Eric 36
Roughton Gill (Glenderaterra) *91,* 93–96, *98–99,* 101, 165
Roughton Gill (High Pike) *113,* 114, *117,* 125
sabre-tooth tiger 165
Saddleback Old Mine 155, *156*
Sandbed Mines 110–111, 125, *129*
Saunders Lakeland Mountain Marathon 123
Scafell / Scafell Pike 9, 13, 16–17, 36, 47, *103,* 109, 125, 140, *159, 167,* 168
Scales (village) 67, 158
Scales Fell *18,* 25, 27, *31–32, 37, 38–39, 63,* 65–66, *70, 77, 79,* 150, *164, 166, 170,* 172
    ascent 1793 27–29
Scales Tarn 9, 12, 16, *25, 26, 27, 31,* 65, 135–136, 165, 172
    Coleridge describes 31
    John Stuart Mill describes 31–32
    Jonathan Otley describes 34
    Julia Bradbury disparages 36
    route described 27
Scaley Beck *77,* 79
Scase, Matthew 172
Scotland, view from *20–21*
Scotland, view to *167*
self-castration 48
Sense and Sensibility (Austen) 29
Sgurr nan Gillean 124
Sharp Edge *2–3, 6,* 9, 12, *13,* 16, *20,* 25, 27, 28, *31, 40–43,* 65, 66, *76,* 79, 86, 100, 137, *150,* 152, 155, *156, 157,* 159, 165, 172, 173
    ascent of 1810 34–35
    J Bradbury ascent 35–36
    route described 36
sheep breeds *77*
Sinen Gill 12, *91, 96,* 100–102
Skiddaw *7,* 9, *21, 22,* 47, 49, 67, 93, *113,* 135, 138, *144,* 157, 165, *166,* 172 see also Bakestall, Dodd, Lonscale Fell
Skiddaw cloth 115
Skiddaw Forest 93, 168
Skiddaw Granite 12, *13,* 34, 96–102, 173
Skiddaw House 93, *97,* 123
    track to 93, *95,* 96, *100, 103*
Skiddaw Slates (Skiddaw System) 9, 13–16, 34, 96, 100–102, 135, *143, 172–173*
Slee, John, prankster 156
Snowdon 34

Snowdon Lily 12
solufluction *141,* 165
Song at the Feast of Brougham Castle (Wordsworth) 136–137
Souther Fell *6, 17, 25,* 109, *121, 133,* 135, 152, *153,* 155–159, *161,* 172
    route described 158–159
    spectral army 12, 156–158
Southey, Robert 31, 51, 173
Spain 1937 (Auden) 55
Spanish Armada 47
spectral army of Souther Fell 12, 156–158
St John's Church *45,* 55–56
St John's Vale *16,* 17, 47, *51, 72,* 93
St Kentigern's Church, Caldbeck 114, *118–119*
St Kentigern's Church, Mungrisdale 156, *160*
Steeple 123, *167*
Stiperstones 156
Strathclyde, Kingdom of 156
summit of Blencathra see Halls Fell Top
Survey of the Lakes (Clarke, 1787) 169
Sustrans C2C bike route 56
Sweden 110
Swinside farm *112,* 123
Tales & Legends (Tuvar, 1852) 49
tank warfare 131
tarns, see Bowscale Tarn, Bright Tarn, Scales Tarn
Tarns of Lakeland (Heaton Cooper) 156
tea strainers, fossil 165
Tertullian 36
Tewet Tarn see Bright Tarn
Thirlmere 13, *45,* 51, *94,* 168
Thorpe Cloud 10
Thought suggested by … Saddleback (Coleridge) 18
Threlkeld *6,* 9, 31, *45,* 47–48, 54–56, *58–59,* 65, 66, 110, 165, 168
Threlkeld Common *11*
Threlkeld Fell 12
Threlkeld granite quarry *45, 88*
Threlkeld Hall *141*
Threlkeld Knotts *88–89, 95*
Threlkeld, Sir Launcelot 137
Tintern Abbey (Wordsworth) 31
To the River Greta (Wordsworth) 54
Tongue, the (Bannerdale) 135, *161*
Tullie House, Carlisle 116
tungsten (wolfram) 17, 125, 131
Tuvar, Lorenzo 49
Tyler, Ian 109–111, 131
Ullswater *16,* 27, *72,* 138, 165
Universe, Djinn of all the 12
Vale of Eden *129–130, 146–147,* 155, *170–171*
Vale of Keswick 7, *22–23,* 44–61, 67, *72, 167,* 168
Valentine, Colin 66
vein breccia *85*
Wainwright summit, dullest 12, 131
Wainwright, A 9, 12, 27, 34, 35–36, 76, 79, 84, 85, 93, 96, 131, 140, 168, 169, *172*
Wales (seen from Blencathra) 168
Walpole, Hugh 47
West, Thomas 51, 54
Wild Eldric 156–157
wolfram, see tungsten
Woodcock Graves, John 115–116, *118*
Wordsworth, William 31, 34, 47, 51,54, 111, 136–137, 157, 173